SCOTLAND'S STAINED GLASS

MAKING THE COLOURS SING

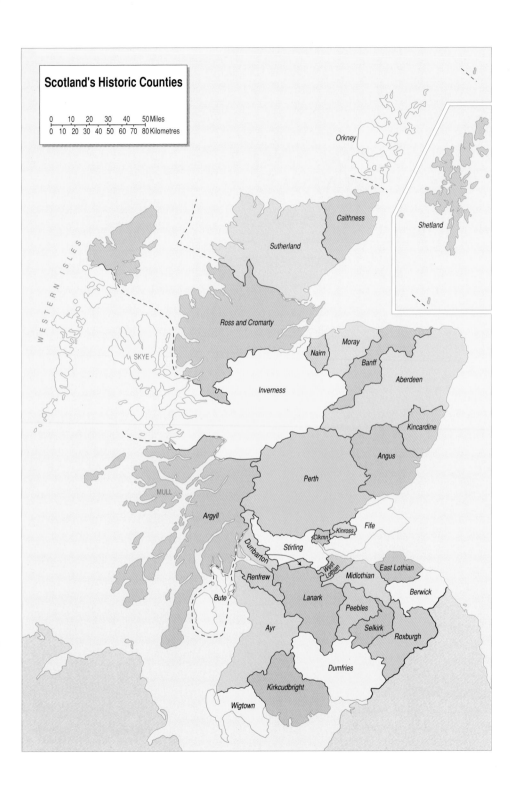

Scotland's Historic Counties

0 10 20 30 40 50 Miles
0 10 20 30 40 50 60 70 80 Kilometres

Orkney

Shetland

WESTERN ISLES

Caithness

Sutherland

Ross and Cromarty

SKYE

Inverness

Nairn

Moray

Banff

Aberdeen

Kincardine

Angus

Perth

MULL

Argyll

Fife

Kinross

Clkmn

Stirling

Dunbarton

West Lothian

Midlothian

East Lothian

Renfrew

Berwick

Bute

Lanark

Peebles

Ayr

Selkirk

Roxburgh

Dumfries

Kirkcudbright

Wigtown

DISCOVERING HISTORIC SCOTLAND

SCOTLAND'S STAINED GLASS

MAKING THE COLOURS SING

MICHAEL DONNELLY

SERIES EDITOR: ALEXANDRA SHEPHERD

HISTORIC SCOTLAND

EDINBURGH: THE STATIONERY OFFICE

ABOUT THE AUTHOR

Michael Donnelly is the leading authority on Scottish stained glass of the 19th and early 20th centuries. From 1972 to 1990 he was Assistant Curator of the People's Palace Museum in Glasgow, where he initiated an intensive programme of research into Glasgow's pivotal role in stained-glass manufacture. He conducted a rescue programme, salvaging glass threatened by demolition and neglect, and built up a significant public collection. Since then he has worked as Project Officer with Dunfermline Heritage Trust and on a number of restoration and preservation projects. He is currently working on a biography of the Scottish designer Daniel Cottier and continuing his programme of research and publication of Scottish stained glass, begun with *Glasgow Stained Glass* and expanded with this volume. He welcomes any information on stained glass and can be contacted via the Smith Art Gallery and Museum, Stirling.

ACKNOWLEDGEMENTS

No work is ever achieved in a vacuum and in the preparation of this volume I have had a host of collaborators in the hundreds of clergy, church officers and worshippers across the denominations, the custodians of private and public institutions, and above all the many private householders who have given me access and permission to photograph and record their glass. I am particularly indebted for much of the information in the first chapter to Sara Brown's excellent general survey of *European Stained Glass* and to Pamela C Graves' unpublished thesis 'Scottish Medieval Stained Glass. The archeological and documentary evidence'.

I am also indebted to the work of fellow researchers Roger Billcliffe, Nicola Gordon Bowe, Jude Burkhauser, John Canning, Peter Cormack, Ian Gow, William Hardie, Martin Harrison, Martin Hopkinson, Juliet Kinchin, Brian Lambie, Jane Lindsay, Clare McGread, Rona Moody, Karen Moon, Professor Virginia Raguin of Boston, George Rawson, Pamela Robertson, Sax Shaw, Dr John Stewart, the late Professor James L Sturm of New York and the late Frank Worsdall. Thanks to Neil Curtis of Aberdeen for helping to wrestle the technology of text transmission and of course to my ever patient and helpful editor, Alexandra Shepherd. Many of the photographs which illustrate this volume would not exist but for the singular generosity of the late Roddy McFarquhar, whose gift of a camera allowed my work to continue.

I have been especially fortunate to be aided by some of the very best librarians and archivists, particularly those of the Mitchell Library, Glasgow, the National Library of Scotland, Edinburgh, and of the Colleges of Art and the university libraries of both Glasgow and Edinburgh. Thanks to the Gillett family for help over many years and long overdue thanks to Irene Pyle and Andrew Pollock of the People's Palace, and, finally, to Elspeth King, my partner, for putting up with – and even sharing – my ongoing obsession.

Cover illustrations: front, *Angel plucking tulips* (detail), Harrington Mann and *Christian struggling with Apollyon*, Sadie McLellan; back, detail of great west window, Broom Parish Church, Ralph Cowan and *Gather ye the Rosebuds*, E A Taylor.

Published by The Stationery Office and available from:
The Stationery Office Bookshops

71 Lothian Road, Edinburgh EH3 9AZ (counter service only)

59-60 Holborn Viaduct, London EC1A 2FD

temporary location until mid-1998 (counter service only)

68-69 Bull Street, Birmingham B4 6AD Tel 0121-236 9696 Fax 0121-236 9699

33 Wine Street, Bristol BS1 2BQ Tel 0117-926 4306 Fax 0117-929 4515

9-21 Princes Street, Manchester M60 8AS Tel 0161-834 7201 Fax 0161-833 0634

16 Arthur Street, Belfast BT1 4GD Tel 01232 238451 Fax 01232 235401

The Stationery Office Oriel Bookshop

The Friary, Cardiff CF1 4AA

Tel 01222 395548 Fax 01222 384347

The Stationery Office publications are also available from:

The Publications Centre (mail, telephone and fax orders only)

PO Box 276 London SW8 5DT

General enquiries 0171-873 0011

Telephone orders 0171-873 9090

Fax orders 0171-873 8200

Accredited Agents

(see Yellow Pages) and through good booksellers

All photographs by Michael Donnelly unless otherwise acknowledged.

The Stationery Office

First published 1997 by The Stationery Office Limited, South Gyle Crescent, Edinburgh, EH12 9EB.

ISBN 0 11 495793 2

British Library Cataloguing in Publication Data

A catalogue record for this book is available from the British Library Applications for reproduction should be made to The Stationery Office Limited

CONTENTS

FOREWORD

Scotland is a country where the imprint of history is still clearly visible in the landscape, in its houses, churches, farmsteads and settlements large and small. All these have coloured, and been coloured by, their setting in mountains or moorland, on fertile pasture or sandy shore, at loch-side or rivermouth. Of paramount importance has always been the all-encompassing influence of the sea, for Scotland is set amidst the searoads of the Celtic provinces in the west and the Scandinavian regions to the north, the trading routes with the mainland of Europe to the east and the land and sea approaches to that dominant neighbour, England, in the south. Scotland's cultural history has thus been moulded by a mixture of influences, fluctuating in importance, absorbed and transformed in ways that are peculiarly Scottish. This series aims to provide a view across the mosaic of that history from its earliest beginnings to the present day; each volume covers one individual aspect of the panorama but the themes are interwoven: kings and queens, heraldry and houses, wars and warriors, stained glass and churches – all link to create a tapestry of Scotland's vigorous past and her historic present.

The history of stained glass in Scotland is a dramatic one. The destruction wrought by the Reformation and its aftermath means that little remains of the windows of the earliest period but that loss is balanced by the explosion of creativity beginning in the 19th century, which produced glass equalling, and in many cases surpassing, anything produced elsewhere in the world. This book charts the progress of stained-glass production through the lives of the men and women whose individual brilliance, skill and determination have left Scotland a rich legacy of the art form at its most stunning. More than a history, this volume is also a cry for the fuller recognition and preservation of what remains of this legacy and a plea for support for today's stained-glass artists, through whom the skills and inventiveness so characteristic of the finest Scottish glass will be taken into the next millennium.

ALEXANDRA SHEPHERD
Series Editor

INTRODUCTION

THE HISTORY AND PRODUCTION
OF STAINED GLASS

Unlike England, which has an extensive literature on the subject, Scottish stained glass generated few contemporary reviews and a mere handful of monographs. Its outstanding exponents were seldom awarded even the most perfunctory of obituaries. This overview will inevitably reflect the unevenness of the surviving material, both the glass itself and the related documents, and its size allows scope only for a certain amount of detail. It is meant as a further step towards a comprehensive history of Scottish stained glass, begun in 1981 with my publication *Glasgow Stained Glass*. I hope it will stimulate a renewed interest in this most neglected – yet most sublime – of architectural arts.

THE HISTORICAL BACKGROUND

Stained glass is a medium where, by the use of coloured glass and the manipulation of transmitted daylight, the interiors of buildings can be not only lit but superbly decorated.

The use of glass, both coloured and plain, in architecture probably had its origins in Ancient Egypt. The introduction of the **blowpipe**, a key breakthrough in glass manufacture, occurred in about the 1st century BC, probably in Syria. The Greeks and the Romans made extensive use of vessel glass and, towards the end of the Roman Empire, window glass, cast rather than blown, was fairly widespread and has been found on many sites throughout Britain.

As an architectural medium, stained glass has existed in western Europe since at least the late 9th century, but came into its own as a major component of church building in the 12th and 13th centuries.

OPPOSITE: *An icon for Scotland by one of Scotland's finest stained-glass artists:* Sir William Wallace, Guardian of Scotland, *by Douglas Strachan, St Margaret's Chapel, Edinburgh Castle.*

The reconstruction by Abbot Suger of the Abbey of **St Denis** on the outskirts of Paris between 1122 and 1151 is generally accepted as marking the beginnings of the Gothic Style in architecture and paved the way for the triumph of medieval stained glass at such French cathedrals as Chartres, Sens and Bourges and in England at Canterbury and York.

Typical stained glass of the 12th and 13th centuries consisted of a mosaic of pieces of individually coloured glass held together by grooved straps of lead known as *calms* (probably another Roman innovation). The glass used was coloured throughout in the molten state and was known as **pot metal** after the clay pots or crucibles in which it was melted.

Flashed glass was introduced about 1250 in order to deal with problems associated with colours like red or ruby, which tended to turn opaque in the firing. It was produced by the glass blower dipping his blowpipe first into a pot of molten white glass and then into a colour so that, when blown, cut, and cooled (annealed), the finished sheet of glass consisted of two distinct layers. The thick or bottom layer was white clear glass while the top thin layer was coloured. By removing part of this top layer by abrasion, a practice introduced in Germany in about 1260, **two colours** could be achieved on the one piece of glass.

Initially the medieval glaziers (who were usually monks) were content to produce windows in which the design was achieved purely by juxtaposition of contrasting colours and leadwork without the use of paint. The earliest surviving leaded glass in Britain of around AD 675 from the Venerable Bede's monastery at Jarrow is of this type. Later, in the 9th century, with the introduction of a dark-brown vitreous paint consisting of a mixture of iron oxide, powdered glass, and a fixative such as honey or gum Arabic, the development of an economic and superbly decorative painted glass began. The application of **yellow stain** – the technical breakthrough which has given a generic name to the entire medium – was not introduced in Europe until about 1300 and only arrived in Britain *c*. 1314. This consisted of applying a mixture of silver nitrate, powdered glass and gum Arabic on to carefully selected portions of the outer face of the glass, which, when fired, produced a range of colour

Medieval fragments of stained glass from the clerestory of Glasgow Cathedral, 13th/14th centuries; discovered during the 19th-century 'restoration' (Historic Scotland).

from pale lemon to deep orange. This had the obvious advantage of enabling the artist, by abrading a piece of flashed glass, to introduce three colours on the one piece, which could then be further enriched by matt painting, cross hatching, stippling and other painting techniques.

The introduction in mid 16th-century Switzerland of new **enamel colours** further extended the range of effects available to the glazier. Each of these technical progressions had profound implications for the style and effect of the stained glass produced. Today by general consensus the finest achievements of medieval stained glass are to be found in the work of the largely anonymous glaziers who created the wonderful 12th- and 13th-century medallion windows of Chartres, St Denis, St Chapelle, Beauvais, Canterbury and York. The quality of their glass (particularly the Chartres magnificent blues, which owe their special qualities to the very haphazard nature and unavoidable pollution of early glass manufacture) remain a marvel which modern science has sometimes approached, perhaps occasionally equalled, but never surpassed.

No one who has personally experienced the awesome interiors of Chartres or St Chapelle would seriously question that judgement. However, as in all spheres of human endeavour, once a technological advance has been achieved it is virtually impossible to advocate the return to a more primitive, if beautiful, one, which has become unfashionable. Thus, as the technological quality of glass production improved, a more elaborate and painterly style developed in tandem, moving progressively away from the two-dimensional quality of the design and the fundamental translucency of colour, which remains the very essence of the medium. By the beginning of the 17th century, the widespread use of enamels and the ever more elaborate striving after complexities of pattern more appropriate to mural and easel painting led to a virtual collapse of confidence in the medium. It was to be some time before that confidence was re-established.

Glass in the Middle Ages

Two types of glass were produced widely in the Middle Ages. The most common was the cylinder or muff, in which a bubble of malleable glass taken up on to the blowpipe was manipulated into a cylinder. This was cut open along its length, reheated and pressed flat into a sheet with characteristic raised edges. In the alternative crown method, the bubble of glass was transferred from the blowpipe to a pontil rod of iron and spun into a disk or crown thicker at the centre with its characteristic 'bull's eye.'

MAKING A STAINED-GLASS WINDOW

The modern process of making a stained-glass window differs only in the nature of the kilns and the types of soldering iron used to join together the lead calms; otherwise, little but the quality of the glass and the use of paper *cartoons* (design patterns) would be unfamiliar to the average medieval glazier. To begin with, a carefully measured cartoon of the intended window or panel to be executed would be drawn on the whitewashed surface of a wooden table. Indicating in charcoal or paint the exact position of each **leadline**, the glazier would carefully sketch in the main painted highlights and

colour code each separate part of the design. Then, having selected and cut each piece of glass, using a red-hot iron (today safely replaced with a diamond cutter), awkward shapes would be finished off using a notched metal rod called a *grozing iron*. Each piece of glass would then be placed in turn on its allotted position and the main painted lines traced through from the drawing below. The painted glass, after being fired, would then be held against the light to ascertain its suitability and, on passing inspection, would be returned to its allotted place on the table before being leaded into position.

According to the German monk Theophilus, medieval glaziers started their leading-up process from the middle, with a figure or some other important feature, and worked outwards. Today, windows are 'built' from the bottom right or left corner; a right

A modern stained-glass studio: Glas.works (Joe Boyle and Yvonne Smith), Glasgow, 1997. Yvonne is removing saddle bars from a leaded glass door panel prior to stripping down and releading the panel; Joe, with farrier's nails in place, in the process of leading up a panel for the Trades House Bar, Dundee.

angle is established by nailing in two laths of wood to hold the work in place as construction proceeds. Each piece of glass is surrounded by the H-section lead calm and held firmly in place by broad-headed **farriers' nails**, while each joint is carefully soldered and fixed. When the entire panel has been leaded up and soldered on one side, it is carefully turned over and the process is repeated on the outside or non-painted face of the glass. After this is completed, both surfaces of the panel or window are scrubbed over with a paste or cement made of whitening, plaster of Paris, white spirit, boiled linseed oil and lamp-black (originally soot). The stiff bristles of the brush help to

push the sludge-like mixture between the lead and the glass so that when hardened a sound waterproof seal is effected.

Finally having determined where the maximum stress points are on the window, the glazier solders a series of copper wires or **ties** at regular intervals across the inner painted face of the glass in regularly spaced bands. The spacing of these bands are different with each window and determine the position of the *saddle bars* of iron, which will support the vertical weight of the window and anchor it firmly to the stone mullions.

Many large medieval **medallion windows** were so complex that specially forged metal support frames known as *ferramenta* were used to support the weight of the numerous individual panels. Where in 19th- or 20th-century large-scale windows this system has been abandoned, the results have been potentially disastrous, and the familiar buckling and bowing of the panels due to internal and external pressure, leading to the break-up of the waterproof seal and the cracking of glass are all too familiar.

THE EARLY HISTORY OF SCOTTISH STAINED GLASS

Not everybody in the medieval Church was happy with the worldly magnificence of Abbot Suger's Abbey of St Denis. St Bernard of Clairvaux's Cistercian Order decreed in 1134 that windows in their abbeys should be of 'clear glass, without colour or cross', intended to avoid ostentation in churches 'where beauty is more admired than sanctity is revered'. The result of this embargo was the development by the Cistercian master glaziers of a new style in which conventionalised foliage, based on elaborate geometric patterns, was executed primarily on silvery white and green glass, relieved with small areas of colour to emphasise specific parts of the design.

This glass, *grisaille*, apart from being more adapted to a contemplative rather than a didactic approach to religious belief, was also significantly cheaper. Compared with England or France, Scotland was a small and relatively poor country, a situation not helped by the constant disruption of its economy and destruction of its religious houses by the seemingly endless strife with its aggressive southern neighbour. It therefore comes as no great surprise that the evidence from recent archaeological investigations, such as those at Jedburgh, on the nature and extent of Scottish medieval glass, reveals that grisaille glass was widely used, apparently with no doctrinal preference, by Benedictines, Augustinians, Dominicans and Franciscans in equal measure. Nonetheless, it is still possible that

The Arms of James V and Mary of Guise by J Rynd, The Magdalene Chapel, Cowgate, Edinburgh, c. 1542.

further excavation at Scottish ecclesiastical sites may provide evidence of the more expensive polychromatic glass so widely used south of the border.

As the earliest history of stained glass is inextricably mixed with that of the Church so its subsequent development and survival was dictated by the events of the 16th and 17th centuries. When in 1560 the Presbyterian Lords of the Council ordered the cleansing of Scotland's kirks of 'all kynd of monuments of idolatyre', they specifically excluded any destruction of the actual fabric of the the buildings such as 'windocks' or 'eyther glass in wark'. Clearly in the first flush of the Reformation little heed was paid to their orders and thousands of stained-glass windows were destroyed. Certainly the choirs of the larger churches and cathedrals, as the focus of the hated mass, were systematically dismantled with only a few outstanding exceptions such as Glasgow Cathedral escaping the wrath of the people. For purely practical reasons, much glass survived in the new kirks until it could be replaced, a process which took many years. Figure windows depicting saints and the Virgin Mary were of course systematically erased. Grisaille, however, was less offensive and it is likely that a great deal of it survived in place into the 17th century. No doubt much that did survive was destroyed during later bouts of sectarian strife. However, other chief factors in its ultimate disappearance were lack of maintenance and loss of skills through the dispersal of the monastic communities which had produced and maintained it.

Apart from the excavated finds and two remarkable collections of medieval glass fragments, uncovered last century at Holyrood Abbey and Glasgow Cathedral, the only Scottish stained glass to have survived the destruction of the Reformation and its aftermath are the four armorial panels intact and *in situ* at the Magdalene Chapel, in Edinburgh's Cowgate, dating from the reign of James V and scarce examples of rondels at Fyvie Castle, Aberdeenshire, and Yester House, Midlothian.

For a fuller picture of the glass of the late Middle Ages and the Renaissance, we have to rely on **written sources**. Royal and ecclesiastical records, fragmentary though they are, have frequent references to glazing schemes. Thus in 1390 the Customers of Linlithgow in the Exchequer Rolls record glass given to the Abbey of Paisley by King Robert II. Royal benefactions were always likely to be of the highest available quality, and it is possible that future excavations at the Abbey might reveal evidence of their type and quality. John Peebles, Bishop of Dunkeld (1378–1390), glazed the east window of his cathedral. Evidence suggests that these were figurative. Other glazing programmes in the chancel by Bishop Robert Cardeny in the early 15th century and in the nave by Bishop Thomas Lauder *c.* 1455 are likely to have been similarly ambitious. The West window at Kinloss Abbey was also glazed by Abbot John Ellem in 1460. The glazing schemes at royal abbeys like Holyrood would be suitably regal, and the Lord High Treasurer's Accounts for November 1478 confirm the presence of 'ane glassenwright' engaged on a programme of repair for Queen Margaret. Similar accounts for the same building also survive from 1552.

When in the late 18th century the French Revolution led to the dispersal of important glass from St Denis, Chartres and other centres, English connoisseurs like Horace Walpole established important collections. However such was the continuing prejudice against 'graven images' in Scotland that the few recycled medieval panels such as those at St Bride's Church, Douglas, Lanarkshire, were only acquired in the late 19th century from redundant English churches rather than from France. Sadly, pioneers of a revival in stained glass like the Irish artist Thomas Jervais, famous for his collaboration with Sir Joshua Reynolds on the windows of Christchurch, Oxford, found little interest; there were no purchasers for his glass transparencies when he held an exhibition in November 1789 in the rooms above Thomas Ruddiman's Bookshop on Edinburgh's South Bridge.

CHAPTER 1

GOTHIC REVIVALS

SCOTTISH STAINED GLASS RESURRECTED

The Romantic movement in literature and the Gothic Revival in architecture were inextricably linked with a widespread intellectual response to the uncertainties created by the industrial revolution. In this chapter we look at the reawakening of interest in medieval architecture and stained glass.

It was not until some 250 years after the Reformation that the first faint rekindling of interest in stained glass began in Scotland. The initiative came in the early 19th century from wealthy high church **Episcopalians**, who, shielded by their status and position, could afford to ignore the displeasure of the Kirk by building and adorning private chapels on their estates. With virtually no indigenous sources to draw upon it is hardly surprising that the earliest of these 19th-century commissions were supplied by the English firm of W Raphael Edginton. This was at Crawford Priory near Cupar, Fife, in 1812 and for the chancel of St John's Episcopal Church, Princes Street, Edinburgh, in 1815.

Stained glass of some kind had re-emerged in a **domestic** setting but this amounted to little more than the thinnest of flashed or etched glass panels in the transoms of doors and even these were few. The style and quality of this glass remains unknown and the loss of so many fine late 18th- and early 19th-century mansions makes it highly unlikely that we shall ever know its extent. However it is probable that it was not dissimilar to the armorial and decorative glass installed and possibly designed by D R Hay for Walter Scott at Abbotsford *c.* 1819.

Given the enormous popularity of Scott's novels and the unchallenged position of Edinburgh as the architectural and literary capital of Scotland, it ought to have been here that here that a 19th-century revival of stained glass should have occurred. However

OPPOSITE: *A fine example of the best of the 19th-century pioneering studios: Gethsemene, Sir Noel Paton for Ballantine & Son, Dunfermline Abbey, c. 1870.*

Sir Walter Scott

The fame of Scott as the inspiration of so much of the Romantic movement in literature was matched by the architectural influence of his house. Its building was just one manifestation of his long-standing competition with his near neighbour Lord Buchan. Buchan had reacquired his ancient property of Dryburgh Abbey from Scott's embarrassed relatives and in so doing had unwittingly acquired the undying dislike of the great novelist who was compelled to look jealously on while Buchan lovingly restored this most romantic of ruins as the centrepiece of his personal estate. Scott's reply was Abbotsford, which he acquired as a farmhouse and began with several architect collaborators to convert and reconstruct into a rival shrine to Scotland's historic and imagined past. His eclectic mix of Gothic, Jacobean and renaissance detail, plundered from the abbeys and castles of Scotland, provided the inspirational compliment to his novels and through Fox Talbot's pioneer photographs became one of the most architecturally influential of all Scottish houses.

Edinburgh was also the headquarters of the national Church, which remained doctrinally opposed to stained glass. Moreover in the early decades of the 19th century, Edinburgh was regarded as the 'Athens of the North' and the classical style in architecture reigned supreme. It would take a generation for Scott's legacy to bear fruit. And it would be a writer of ballads and songs who would be in its vanguard.

PIONEERING DAYS: JAMES BALLANTINE

James Ballantine was born in Edinburgh in 1808 and began his career – like many other stained-glass artists – by training as a house painter and decorator. This involved anything from five to seven years' apprenticeship, starting as the lowly slab boy cleaning the brushes for the journeymen, and grinding the colours. Ballantine was lucky in so far as he became a slab boy to the great Scottish topographical artist David Roberts, whose paintings first conveyed to Scottish audiences the glamour and mystique of Ancient Egypt. We do not know where Ballantine acquired his knowledge of glass staining. It is most likely that he spent some time in an English studio, perhaps at Newcastle, before establishing his own firm in 1837 at the age of 29.

By 1845 he was confident and established enough in the trade to publish a slim volume entitled *A Treatise on Painted Glass,* which was the first Scottish text on the subject in modern times. In this work he enthusiastically advocated the use of stained glass in domestic interiors and was highly critical of the indiscriminate copying of medieval glass.

Viewed from the advantage of hindsight, Ballantine's own work as a glass painter cannot be placed in the first rank, and was often with some justice condemned by his contemporaries. Nevertheless, he was an excellent **talent spotter**, and adopted the commendable practice of sponsoring his apprentices for the design classes of the Trustees' Academy.

If Ballantine had been depending upon Scottish commissions in his early career it is unlikely that his business would have survived. However, in 1843, his sample panel was selected as the winning entry in the national competition for the stained glass for the **House of Lords**. Much of his work was done for English clients. His House of Lords commission secured him work in England and Denmark. His earliest surviving design in Scotland appears to be for the Episcopal Chapel of the Eremite at Murthly in Perthshire (1846).

His first important secular commission in Scotland came the following year when he executed designs for four armorial windows in the newly completed Scott Monument in Princes Street, Edinburgh. The cartoons were provided by his former employer and friend David Roberts.

It was not until 1856 that Ballantine secured his first stained-glass commission from the Church of Scotland as part of the ongoing restoration of **Old Greyfriars** in Edinburgh, which had been severely damaged by fire. Then came another for the Sandyford/Henderson Church in Glasgow. Both these commissions were probably consolation prizes awarded as a result of what was widely perceived as an affront to national pride over the *cause célèbre* of the reglazing of Glasgow Cathedral, one of the stormiest architectural controversies of the 19th century.

GLASGOW CATHEDRAL: THE MUNICH GLASS CONTROVERSY

In response to propaganda by Archibald McLellan, Glasgow's ancient cathedral had been 'improved', by extensive remodelling and the demolition of its western towers. James Ballantine, consulted on the feasibility of installing stained glass in the great east window, seized the opportunity and provided a sketch design (probably by the artist John Faed), pricing the job at £400. The design was approved. During one of his visits to the cathedral to discuss its erection, Ballantine met by chance Sir Andrew Orr, the Lord Provost. Ballantine succeeded in persuading the provost that it was his duty to set an example for the rest of the city's leading citizens by commissioning a window. Again the artist produced a sketch design which was eagerly approved by the provost, who had also persuaded several of his friends to subscribe for more.

Fearing that the project might escalate out of control, Ballantine offered to draw up a **general scheme** for the entire building in order to prevent a repetition of subjects and to maintain an overall unity of design. This offer was favourably received and Ballantine set about his task only to be confronted on his return by a 'Committee

Ballantine the Renaissance man

Not purely a visual artist, Ballantine also enjoyed a status within Edinburgh's cultural scene through his literary activities. He was widely recognised as a leading authority on Robert Burns and, from the early 1830s, he contributed songs and poems to the Scotsman, collecting and publishing them in monthly parts from 1843 as 'The Gaberlunzie's Wallet'. His songs 'Bonnie Bonaly', 'Ilka Blade o' Grass' and 'Castles in the Air' were among the most popular songs of the time.

OPPOSITE: Christ and the Woman of Samaria, *Ballantine & Allen, Ibrox Parish Church, 1865.*

of Superintendence', composed of the great and good with Charles Heath Wilson as its secretary and artistic advisor.

Wilson was a confirmed devotee of the hybrid enamelled glass then being produced by the **Royal Bavarian Glassworks** at Munich. His own teaching experience at the Trustees' Academies in Edinburgh and Glasgow and the poor performance of British studios at the Great Exhibition of 1851 had convinced him of the superiority of this German school, whose cartoonists were artists of national standing. In this prejudice he was firmly supported by Charles Winston (1814–1865), an English barrister, whose monumental two-volume study of medieval glass had made him the leading authority on the subject.

A panel of Munich stained glass, Glasgow Cathedral, c. 1856.

Wilson had already made up his mind that if possible the entire scheme should be awarded to Munich. However, in order to convince waverers on his committee, squeeze Ballantine out, and forestall the inevitable criticism from the architectural press, he instituted an inquiry into the current state of British stained glass. A questionnaire was sent to almost every active stained-glass studio asking for estimates for the Glasgow Cathedral project and a list of previous works to be inspected by delegates from the committee. Letters were also sent to leading architects and designers eliciting their opinions. With the notable exception of Charles Winston, they were virtually unanimous in their **opposition** to the use of Munich glass: ignoring this, Wilson and his committee proceeded to place the commission with Munich. David Kier, the head of one of Glasgow's pioneer stained-glass studios, as master glazier for the cathedral, was caught in the middle of this row and had the unenviable if profitable job of installing the reviled scheme.

In Scotland the natural disappointment at the loss of such an important commission quickly turned to fury, when in self-justification Wilson issued an officious public report in which he attacked British stained glass as inferior to that of Munich. In a patriotic reaction to this pronouncement, **Henry Houldsworth**, the powerful textile manufacturer and one of the principal subscribers, broke ranks and placed the commission for his window with Ballantine. Sadly Houldsworth was to die before its completion and the window was again rejected.

The Glasgow Architectural Society, which had not been consulted, chose the occasion of the installation of great West window designed by Moritz von Schwind to vent their collective disapproval. Public opinion forced Wilson and his committee to compromise and all of the rejected British studios who were still interested were invited to install windows in the lower church.

The aftermath

In the end Ballantine benefited by an injured national pride and the commissions for Greyfriars and Sandyford broke the dam of Presbyterian resistance to stained glass. Henceforth Ballantine's studio was able to secure a whole series of important commissions beginning with a scheme at Trinity Church, Dean, Edinburgh (1858). Ballantine's rejected Houldsworth window was installed with much pomp in St Mark's Church, Anderston, in February 1862 and shortly afterwards commissions for windows at the Old Kirk, Ayr, and South Bantaskine House, Falkirk (now in the new Falkirk Shopping Centre), followed in April. This increased business meant that Ballantine needed to recruit additional staff and among several new apprentices who joined his studio were **Stephen Adam** and his future partner, **David Small**.

Ballantine's best work includes the windows for St John's Episcopal Church, Princes Street, Edinburgh, dating from the mid 1850s, the fine sequence of windows c. 1863 in Ibrox Parish Church, Glasgow, and the important group of windows in Dunfermline Abbey dating from 1873–1879. Of note is the *Agony in the Garden* (1879), a pictorial and rather beautiful window designed by Noel Paton; and the very different and splendid great West window of 1882, also by Paton, featuring portraits of Queen Margaret, King Malcolm Canmore, William Wallace and Robert the Bruce.

The great west window, Dunfermline Abbey, Sir Noel Paton for James Ballantine & Son, 1882.

Unlike most of the other commercial studios of the 19th century, Ballantine's reputation rested almost exclusively on ecclesiastical glass. In this area his

James Ballantine II

Alexander Ballantine was succeeded by his son, James, who, in spite of modernising his palette considerably, never quite escaped the pictorial style of his father. He was the first Scot to broadcast on radio (1925) on his subject. His finest windows were probably the twelve apostles scheme for Christ Church Cathedral, Victoria, British Columbia, Canada, in 1929.

most prestigious commission in Scotland was unequivocally the scheme of windows installed in **St Giles' Kirk** in Edinburgh. Ballantine certainly regarded it as a vindication of his reputation and employed the artist Robert Herdman, a leading historical painter, to design the cartoons.

After his death in 1877 he was succeeded by his son **Alexander**, whose strong figure composition and lighter colour schemes were to give the firm a new lease of life with hundreds of technically competent if rather traditional windows to his credit and that of his partner, Gardiner. Alexander also lectured frequently on the subject of stained glass, a measure of the craft's growing respectability. One of his finest efforts is the comprehensive scheme on the life of St Cuthbert for St Cuthbert's Parish Church, Edinburgh.

OTHER LEADING STUDIOS

James Ballantine was not without his rivals in the capital and, as well as Daniel Cottier (see Chapter 2), healthy competition was forthcoming from the early 1850s from the studio of **Francis**

Barnett of Leith. Barnett was a third generation glazier from York, where his grandfather and his father, John Joseph Barnett had both worked as glass makers for the firm of Prince & Prest. In the early 1840s, J J Barnett and his three sons branched out into glass staining. They were involved in 'restoring' (effectively duplicating) several medieval windows in York. Francis Barnett was a fully fledged glass stainer by 1844, when, during the visit of the British Association, he displayed an 8ft-high window for All Saints Church in North Street, York.

Two years later, on his father's retiral, the firm broke up and Francis headed for Leith in the company of a Mr Maycock, brother-in-law to Barnett's early patron J A Hansom (inventor of the Cab) and, like himself, a Catholic. Failing to establish a school for ecclesiastical art workers at Leith, Maycock moved on to Birmingham, but Francis Barnett persevered and in a few years had established an extensive business with studio premises. Examples of Barnett's earliest Scottish-made glass can be seen in in Old Greyfriars Church, where doctrinal reticence excluded figures and confined the design to medieval-inspired **geometric ornamental** patterns. More adventurous and much more

confident are the two very large windows commissioned in 1864 for Broughton/St Mary's Parish Church, Edinburgh. Each consists of geometric panels of ornamental glazing with centrepieces depicting John the Baptist and St Paul. For these windows Barnett not only successfully beat off competition from Ballantine but also from Field & Allen's new glass-staining workshop run by Daniel Cottier. In the following year he secured a prestigious overseas commission for 35 windows to be installed in Alloa Roman Catholic Church, Port Elizabeth, South Africa.

The great west window, St Mary Star of the Sea Roman Catholic Church, Leith, F Barnett & Son, c. 1878.

In the 1870s Barnett was joined by his son, William Collinridge Barnett, and perhaps the most comprehensive scheme of glass by the firm can be seen in St Mary's Star of the Sea Roman Catholic Church, opposite their former studio in Constitution Street, Leith. Here the great west window and two re-sited chancel windows in this much altered church by E W Pugin and J A Hansom reveal the remarkably rich, sombre and unusual colour schemes and figure work of their mature studio style. Perhaps the finest window yet identified by this firm is the three-light window depicting Christ in Majesty in Rowand Anderson's Catholic Apostolic Church, Edinburgh. Its powerful composition and sophisticated handling of strong colour make it a worthy companion to the later mural scheme by **Phoebe Traquair**.

OPPOSITE: St Matthew, *Francis Barnett, Broughton/St Mary's Church, Edinburgh, 1865.*

CHAPTER 2

GLASGOW

SECOND CITY OF EMPIRE AND FIRST CITY OF GLASS

The fortunes of stained glass as an architectural art form were intimately bound up in the future of the Church and industry. In 19th-century Glasgow both underwent a revolutionary transformation.

This chapter looks at the talented new exponents of stained glass in Glasgow from the 1860s. The city that had made its fortune in the transatlantic trade in tobacco, sugar and slaves now diversified its capital into the burgeoning new industries of textiles and civil and marine engineering. As the city burst its old boundaries and the wealthy middle classes moved west to avoid the disease and overcrowding of a swelling population, the social pressures inside the national Church came to a head with the **Disruption** of 1843. The new programme of church building which followed this crisis gave a boost to the infant stained-glass industry, which was sustained by speculative housing and the growth of shipbuilding.

In Glasgow, as in Edinburgh, pioneering firms like William Cairney & Sons (1828–1877) Hugh Bogle & Co (1850–1865) and David Kier & Sons (1851–1864) had been able to execute only the most rudimentary domestic and church glazing. Decoration (where it was permitted at all) was confined to embossed glass, which was considered unobtrusive and was of course colourless. Great ornamentalists like **Alexander Thomson** were resourceful in their exploitation of even these limited sources, and his characteristic designs for **embossed glass,** like his cast iron, can be found in many buildings with which he had no direct connection. It was only in the early 1860s that the second generation of these pioneering firms began to execute stained glass worthy of the name.

GLASGOW STUDIOS OF THE 1860S

W & J J Kier

The profits accumulated by David Kier from his lengthy contract installing the Munich glass in Glasgow Cathedral enabled his two

OPPOSITE: *Glass as part of a great decorative scheme:* Love and Audacity, *Daniel Cottier, Cairndhu House, Helensburgh, 1873. One of the landmarks in Cottier's collaboration with Glasgow architect William Leiper.*

IN MEMORY OF CHARLES RANDOLPH

BORN AT STIRLING JUNE 22 1809

DIED AT GLASGOW NOV 11 1878

The Marriage Feast at Cana, W & J J Kier, Holy Rude Church, Stirling, 1878.

sons, William and James, to set up their own studio in 1865. Like James Ballantine and Francis Barnett, their earliest work was modelled on medieval medallion windows featuring small figure panels set on backgrounds of ornamental diamond quarries with elaborate floral borders, in which flashed ruby features prominently. Their earliest style is best seen in Kilmarnock Old Parish Church, where there are a number of fine windows of the 1860s.

Both brothers were involved with their father in the lengthy installation process at the cathedral and their frequent visits to Munich inevitably had a deep impression on them: although they ultimately rejected the Munich enamel processes, their style of the 1870s and 1880s became increasingly pictorial. Among the fine examples of this mature style are their superbly executed *The Marriage Feast at Cana* in Holy Rude Church, Stirling (1878), the large ornamental west window of Alloway Parish Church, the windows in the former Adelaide Street Church (now an arts centre and restaurant) in Bath Street, Glasgow, and the richly detailed Letter of Guildry windows in the Merchant's House of Glasgow (1877–8).

About the end of the 1870s, William Kier junior began designing for the firm, particularly for domestic work. His style is lighter, and his decorative ideas are clearly influenced by the work of Heaton,

Butler and Bayne and some of the other progressive English studios. A fine range of his glass has survived in Rawcliffe Lodge, the former mansion of A B Stewart, the Glasgow millionaire warehouseman, in Mansion-house Road, Cathcart.

John Cairney & Co

John Cairney, according to a family tradition, acquired his training in stained glass at **York Minster**. A more likely explanation is that he worked for Francis Barnett in Edinburgh, who had worked in York Minster and continued to execute important commissions in England long after his establishment at Leith. Whatever the case, Cairney's original role was primarily as an interior decorator and it was only towards the end of the 1850s that his glass embossing and general glazing work had expanded sufficiently for him to employ his friend and client

Raphael, *William Kier Junior, Rawcliffe Lodge, Langside, Glasgow,* c. 1880.

Alexander Thomson to design him a customised studio at 42 Bath Street in 1860. By then his decorating and glass staining activities had provided a launching pad for several talented apprentices, including **John Lamb Lyon**, **Charles Gow** and, most importantly, **Daniel Cottier**.

DANIEL COTTIER: A GREAT INNOVATOR AND THE COMPANY HE KEPT

Daniel Cottier was born in Anderston, Glasgow, in 1838 and at the age of 14 was apprenticed to John Cairney & Co to learn the trade of decorating, glass staining and embossing. Cottier quickly demonstrated a natural aptitude for colour which marked him out as one of Cairney's most promising employees. It was probably towards the end of his apprenticeship that he began to accompany his employer on some of his long-distance jobs to towns like Dunfermline, where a local stained-glass artist **Robert Boyle Watson** acted as an agent for Cairney's glass.

After leaving Cairney, Cottier worked for a time in Edinburgh, perhaps for James Ballantine, while attending evening classes at the

Miriam, *Daniel Cottier,
Dowanhill Parish
Church, Glasgow, 1867.
This figure, though still
somewhat forced in its
handling, points the way
ahead towards Cottier's
mature style. Her
amazonic proportions
owe much to Greek
archaic sculpture and
eschew entirely the
doleful languor so
dominant in the work of
Burne-Jones and his
PreRaphaelite disciples.*

Trustees' Academy. In 1859 he moved to London, where he did the round of the decorative trade, working possibly with fellow apprentice John Lamb Lyon at Ward & Hughes before joining Morris, Marshall, Faulkner & Co in 1861.

Cottier's familiarity with the artwork of the **William Morris studio** at this time was revealed in 1870 when he drew upon the unpublished Morris–Burne-Jones panel *The Lady of Woodbank and her daughters*, executed in 1861 for Woodbank House, Arden, near Bingley, Yorkshire, as a source for his Speirs Memorial window in Paisley Abbey.

In 1862 he returned to Edinburgh, where he secured the post of foreman designer of the established family firm of Field & Allan of Leith. Field's money had been made in the slate industry and the emphasis of the firm was on general building, glazing and slater work. In a very short time Cottier established an up-to-date decorating and stained-glass workshop.

His style as an ornamentalist and colourist was already distinctive and recognisable, and his earliest known commission, for Peddie and Kinnear's Pilrig Parish Church, Leith Walk (1863), reveals a confidence of style remarkable for a 25-year-old. This virtually complete scheme for Field & Allan consists of a series of contrasting **geometric widows** based on a combination of medieval-style grisaille and the rich colours of the medallion window.

Cottier's next major commission came in early 1865. He was selected as the decorator and general glazier for J J Stevenson's Townhead Parish Church on Garngad Hill, Glasgow, a site chosen to dominate the proposed location of a new public park. The church was a bold exercise in **Normandy Gothic**, with a soaring spire making it the most prominent landmark in the north of the city.

In order to combat its hostile industrial environment, Stevenson and Cottier opted for a full polychromatic scheme of decoration of a kind not seen in Scotland since medieval times. The interior of this church was decorated in **distemper colours**, beginning at pew level with a rich warm terracotta ashlar work, divided by stencilled string courses of cream, ornamented with gold stencils. The undersides of the galleries were a light sky blue, while above gallery level the walls were painted a rich cream, the ashlar work and stencils in terracotta,

King David, Daniel Cottier, formerly in Crathie Parish Church, Aberdeenshire, 1873 (now People's Palace collection, Glasgow).

and ornaments in pale blue, Venetian red and gold. Finally the ceiling was painted a deep, almost navy, blue and studded with stars and golden palmettes.

The stained glass that Cottier provided marked a significant advance over Pilrig, particularly in the north rose window, where his broad muscular plant motifs in blue, green, red and yellow provided a perfect foil for the painted decoration which surrounded it. Ironically Cottier was denied the opportunity of complete control when the great south window was awarded to Morris & Co.

The critical reception for Townhead was overwhelmingly favourable and, as a result, Cottier received many other commissions for decoration and glass. The first of these was for Alexander Thomson's important villa, **Holmwood**, in Cathcart.

Cottier's connection with the Glasgow architect **William Leiper** was a long and fruitful one, beginning with a French Gothic villa for William Denny at Kirktonhill in Dumbarton, where he supplied a scheme of stained glass and possibly decoration. In 1867 he also supplied stained glass for Leiper's very distinctive Scotto-Japanese villa, **Woodside**, at Loch Goil. The glass for this house features the earliest surviving examples of what became a house style for Cottier's domestic glass, and consisted of panels made up of decorated square quarries of antique glass varying in colour from pale green to light amber as a setting for elaborate jewel-like monograms of the client's initials or coats of arms.

At the same time Cottier was preparing a scheme of decoration for Leiper's most important commission, a new church for the United Presbyterian congregation at **Dowanhill** in Glasgow. Leiper,

Cottier and the Morris Studio

Cottier had probably heard of William Morris's ideas about changing the face of contemporary decoration when he attended classes given by Morris, Maddox Brown and John Ruskin at the Working Men's College in the East End. It is well known that Morris kept an open house for large numbers of talented volunteers, and Cottier would be only too well aware of the advantage to be derived from understudying such a remarkable group of designers. The studio produced many superb designs for stained glass with Morris, Edward Burne-Jones, Dante Gabriel Rossetti, Philp Webb and Ford Maddox Brown all contributing to the design pool while Morris supervised the general ornamentation, colour schemes and glass painting.

Cottier's expansion

The pace of Cottier's career began to speed up when he married the boss's daughter and opened up his own studio in George Street. Cottier was already thinking of moving to Glasgow, where his former contacts in the trade could work to his advantage. It was probably no accident that his studio, formerly occupied by the bohemian artist and decorator Sam Bough, was next door to the Edinburgh office of Campbell Douglas & Stevenson, one of the most prolific Glasgow architectural firms. The establishment in Hugh Bogle's old premises of the new firm of W & J J Kier left David Kier's old workshops in Carrick Street Anderston vacant; Cottier seized the opportunity and in late 1865 opened his Glasgow branch. He continued to keep an office in Edinburgh until at least 1869.

Justice, *Daniel Cottier, the Advocates' Hall, Aberdeen, 1872.*

like Cottier, was determined to make an impression with his first major church commission, and wanted to further the revolution in church decoration which had begun at Townhead.

The scheme combined walls of a rich terracotta red, dark brown, cream and black, with arabesques in blue, green, vermilion, yellow and black, and a ceiling painted a deep blue with stars and planets. The lavish decoration was also applied to the pulpit screen, the minister's cathedra-like seat, and even the collecting dishes. The painted decoration of the Pulpit Seat was restored by the author and is now in the collection of the People's Palace Museum.

The glass which complemented this tour de force consisted of tall lancets of stylised foliage in repeat geometric patterns. Nothing but the finest antique glass was employed in the now familiar palette of red, pale blue, light green, yellow and amber. In addition to this work the **quatrefoil** tops of the windows below the balcony each contained the head of a biblical woman, such as Ruth or Naomi. Cottier also provided an important two-light window for the choir balcony depicting King David and Miriam.

Cottier's decorative scheme for Alexander Thomson's lost masterpiece, Queen's Park United Presbyterian Church in Glasgow, firmly established him as the most original decorator in Scotland. His regular connection with Thomson was interrupted only by the latter's death, and Leiper continued to work with him on and off for the rest of his life. The chief landmarks of this latter collaboration are **Cornhill House**, Biggar (1869–73), **Col Earn House** at Auchterarder (1870–71) and **Cairndhu House**, Helensburgh (1872–3) (see Chapter frontispiece).

Cottier opened new headquarters in London in 1869 and branches in New York and Sydney in 1873. He decorated and installed expensive stained glass in the **East Kirk of St Nicholas** in

Further Cottier work in Aberdeen: the Jamieson Memorial, St Machar's Cathedral, 1873 (cartoon possibly inspired by the work of Matthew Maris).

Aberdeen, which was sadly destroyed by fire the following year. Soon after, ill health made him turn to art dealing, with firms in London and New York; he spent the remainder of his short life (he died at the age of 53 in 1891) introducing the **Aesthetic movement** in interior design into America and Australia, and in the process establishing a critical new market for contemporary art in Scotland and America. His studio continued to produce glass to his designs long after his untimely death.

THE COTTIER LEGACY: STEPHEN ADAM

Cottier was not only a great decorator, he was a first-rate teacher and one of his finest pupils was **Stephen Adam**. He was born near Edinburgh in 1848 and received his early education at Canonmills School (where his classmates included **Robert Louis Stevenson**). His artistic ability was noted early and encouraged by his parents and teachers, and he was apprenticed to the Edinburgh firm of decorators and stained-glass artists, Ballantine & Allan.

Like most of Ballantine's apprentices, Adam was sponsored by the firm as a student of the Trustees' Academy, but his stay with both was comparatively short. By 1864 he had moved to Glasgow with his parents and in the following year, as a student of the Haldane Academy (Glasgow School of Art), he was awarded a silver medal for the best design for a stained-glass panel. This early mark of success brought him to the attention of Daniel Cottier, who recruited him as one of his assistants towards the end of that year. He later recorded his debt to Cottier:

Peace, *Stephen Adam, c. 1876 (Glasgow University collection).*

In design I have been greatly influenced by the works of Rossetti, Burne-Jones, William Morris and Puvis de Chavannes; and, if I may speak confidently of my work as a Colourist, in Colour I found my master in the late Daniel Cottier, the eminent glass painter.

Adam was accustomed to date his career as a glass painter and designer to 1866. This probably refers to the completion of his apprenticeship and confirms that as a qualified journeyman he would have played a role in such important commissions as **Holmwood House**, **Dowanhill Church**, and **Queen's Park Church** for Alexander Thomson.

When, in 1869, Cottier moved to London, it is evident that there was much work still outstanding on the studio books in Scotland. The completion of this seems to have been entrusted to Adam and Andrew Wells. By 1870 both men felt able to make the crucial break with Cottier and strike out on their own. There is no evidence that this separation was the cause of any rancour between Cottier and his old assistants; on the contrary Cottier had a remarkable ability to maintain friendships with his ex-employees, even when they were operating in competition. In this happy disposition lay the key to his great success in maintaining much of his business in Scotland even after his move to the metropolis.

Stephen Adam's first independent studio (1870) was established in partnership with **David Small**. The partnership ended in 1885 when Small moved to Dundee (where for 30 years he was the chief illustrator to the Dundee *Advertiser*).

It was with **Andrew Wells** that Adam now began to work in a regular if quite informal partnership and much of his best work of the 1870s as a designer and decorator was a product of this collaboration. Andrew Wells trained at the Trustees' Academy before joining Daniel Cottier at Field & Allen. He was Cottier's **chief assistant** on all his Scottish commissions prior to 1869.

Adam's earliest surviving stained-glass scheme is that executed in 1874 for the refurbished 18th-century parish church of St Andrews in Glasgow, the commission for which was divided between Adam & Wells after open competition. The resulting scheme was widely applauded throughout the trade and, in 1914, when an ill thought-out scheme drastically altered Wells's decoration, it was still revered enough to provoke outrage in the columns of the *Journal of Decorative Art*. The surviving elements of Adam's stained-glass scheme, particularly the two figurative designs beneath the south balcony, show Adam as still very much under the influence of Cottier.

It was not until 1877, when he and Wells again teamed up to decorate the newly built Belhaven Parish Church in the Hillhead district of Glasgow for the architect **James Sellars**, that Adam was, for the first time, completely his own master in his ecclesiastical designs. His independence of style and thought was accelerated by a tour of England, France and Belgium studying medieval and modern stained glass. Visits to London and Paris also brought him into direct contact with the work of **Edward Burne-Jones**, **Holman Hunt** and others whose combinations of Neoclassical figure painting and aesthetic decorative style were irresistible. Holman Hunt and **Albert Moore** were particularly influential in his domestic work of this period, and one set of figure panels, now lost or destroyed, formerly in the house of the Rowatt family in Paisley, included a literal translation into glass of Moore's famous painting, *The Shuttlecock*.

Like his old master Daniel Cottier, Adam was by this time fully smitten by the stylistic **influence of Japanese art**. In the great east window at Belhaven he combines panels of Japanese-style foliage, quarries and sunflowers with subtly coloured figure panels based on Sir John Everett Millais' famous illustrations of the Parables from the popular magazine *Good Words*. This celebrated series of illustrations was almost as popular as Holman Hunt's painting *The Light of the World* as a subject for stained glass. Cottier himself produced at least three versions: two in America and one at Bothwell Old Parish Church.

Wells's complementary decoration could not have been more elaborate and he produced a **magnificent scheme** which deliberately invited comparison with the nearby Dowanhill Church. As in so many other churches of this period, the wall decoration has been completely painted out, but the remarkable ceiling with its elaborate symbols of the Evangelists still conveys to any visitor the splendour of the complete scheme.

In 1877 Adam produced his first publication, *Stained Glass – its History and Modern Development*. In this personal manifesto, Adam, like Ballantine before him, ridiculed the widespread practice of making

The Glassblower, Stephen Adam, Maryhill Burgh Hall, 1878 (Glasgow Museums, The People's Palace). In this outstanding series of panels, Adam chose to depict the tradesmen not artificially in their Sunday best as did so many contemporary photographs, but at labour in their working clothes. The accuracy of detail leaves little doubt that the preliminary sketches for these panels were done in the field years before anyone had heard of the Glasgow Boys and in the kind of industrial settings which they avoided like the plague.

slavish copies of earlier styles, so that the country was 'overrun with Stock saints and evangelists'. Appalled by the fakery indulged in by the commercial firms who manufactured these 'deformities', patrons had turned in despair to the 'more captivating German Productions, which at least gives them composition not wanting in devout feeling and well drawn expressive features and drapery. As has been well said they prefer Art without transparency to transparency without art.'

Following the success of his publication, Stephen Adam began one of the most important commissions of his career. This involved designing a complete scheme of stained glass for a new Burgh Hall and Court at **Maryhill** to the north-west of Glasgow. Because of its proximity to the Forth and Clyde Canal, Maryhill had developed a wide range of industries which were the source of its new-found prosperity. Stephen Adam's challenge was to celebrate these industries in a series of 20 square stained-glass panels flanking either side of the main hall. In fulfilment of this challenge he produced a remarkable sequence of images, each depicting a specific trade such as glass blowing, engineering, bleaching, chemical and gas works, bricklaying, iron moulding, and so on. Both the subject matter of the scheme and its treatment were unique.

This is not to say that there are no precedents for Adam's designs in other media. The genre paintings and sketches of **David Allan**, **Walter Geckie**, **David Wilkie**, and above all, **George Harvey** (who occasionally designed for James Ballantine) are relevant and pertinent influences to which Adam, growing up in Edinburgh, was bound to be exposed. But their subject matter is primarily of the old rural Scotland which was already fast disappearing, whereas Adam was concerned to record the urban environment, with its new industries, and the men and women who sustained them.

NEW STAFF AND COLOUR COMBINATIONS

From 1880 Stephen Adam's studio went through a period of expansion. The amount of executed work which survives from this period implies a significant staff of assistants. Unfortunately the loss or dispersal of records has left us with little information as to their identities. An exception is **Joseph Miller**.

Miller, aged 33 when he joined the studio, was only three years younger than Adam and was a skilled glass painter and cartoonist. He was born in 1845 in Newcastle-on-Tyne. His father and grandfather also worked in the local glass industry and his mother was from a glass-making family. He worked for a time in Edinburgh with the decorator J B Bennet, but by 1877 he was in Glasgow working for Adam. His signature, etched with a diamond, can be found on a

*Tidings of Great Joy,
Joseph Miller, Whiteinch
Methodist Church, c.
1886 (People's Palace
collection, Glasgow).
Miller appears to have
remained with Adam's
studio until 1886 when
he established his own
workshop at 330 St
Vincent Street. His
daughter Anne Catherine
Miller (born 1868)
became his apprentice
and worked beside him
till her marriage in
1894.*

*Cleopatra, Stephen
Adam, The Knowe,
Pollokshields, Glasgow,
1890.*

parcel in the panel depicting the Railway Porter with the label 'Newcastle-Maryhill' on the Maryhill Burgh Hall windows.

Another apprentice in Adam's studio at this time was **William Meikle Junior**. The full strength of the studio was probably around twelve, including apprentices. Following the success of the Maryhill job other commissions came thick and fast.

Adam now began a long-term connection with the wealthy congregation of Pollokshields Parish Church, Glasgow, by executing three two-light windows for the west side of the church. The subjects included a reuse of the Nativity design from Alloway and *Charity* (from the Royal Infirmary), continuing the innovations of the previous year. These windows make a dramatic contrast to the more traditional work of W & J J Kier in the same church. Again, architectural canopies are replaced by aesthetic style panels of conventionalised flowers. The main figure panels, particularly that of the *Madonna and Child* and *Charity*, are superbly decorative with only the finest antique glasses being used.

In the early 1880s Adam experimented with an ever richer palette of new glasses as he strove to improve not only the quality of his materials but to control and harmonise them. By the end of the decade he had achieved a new vitality and purity of colour which placed his glass among the best of its kind and confirmed his place as the true successor to Daniel Cottier, and

Galleon, *Robert Burns for Stephen Adam & Son, c.1891 (Private collection, Kelvinside, Glasgow).*

Scotland's foremost artist in stained glass, a position he only relinquished with his death in 1910. Some of the very finest work of this mature period can be seen at Largs at the **Clark Memorial Church**. In the nearby parish church of St Columba, his great transept window is favourably contrasted with a huge west window by Cottier.

For the owners of Alexander Thomson's villa 'The Knowe', Pollokshields, he satisfied his client's Egyptian enthusiasms by designing a Cleopatra door panel (opposite) of such sumptuous richness that Cottier himself would have envied it. By 1896, with a vastly increased workload to contend with, Adam must have been relieved to add

Plenty, *Stephen Adam Junior, c. 1903 (Private collection, Woodside, Glasgow).*

'& son' to his brass plate when **Stephen Junior** graduated from Glasgow School of Art and became his partner. Adam was already employing a number of other artists as freelance designers in an attempt to cope with the huge workload and keep pace with potential rivals.

In 1896 a revised edition of his pamphlet on stained glass entitled *Truth in Decorative Art, Stained Glass, Medieval and Modern* appeared with a remarkable japonaise cover by the brilliant young Edinburgh designer **Robert Burns**, a protégé of **Sir Patrick Geddes** (1854–1932). To date, only one church window by Burns for Adam has been identified: *The Good Samaritan* in Longforgan Parish

Painting, Stephen Adam Junior, Studio Panel, c. 1905 (Glasgow Museums: The People's Palace). Like Gauld, Stephen Adam Junior was probably happiest designing for domestic situations as in his charming panels based on the nursery rhyme Sing a Song of Sixpence *in the Imperial Bar, Howard Street, Glasgow. Several jobs for his short-lived studio,* The Crafts, *came via his friend Charles Rennie Mackintosh and included a stained-glass screen for the Dutch Kitchen Tearoom, Argyle Street, Glasgow, and a scheme for Pettigrew & Stephens' restaurant, Sauchiehall Street. This small panel* Painting *probably comes from this latter commission and is now in the People's Palace collection.*

Church, near Dundee. On stylistic grounds it is likely that he was also responsible for the three small figurative panels in the conservatory screen of Walter McFarlane's House at 21 Park Circus (now the Registry Office) in Glasgow and the small overmantle glass mosaics and panels which adorn several of the rooms. The glass mosaic portraying two girls reading from an open book bears the inscription 'I was painted by Stephen Adam'. This is no doubt literally true, since Robert Burns was not a glass painter and appears to have supplied his designs from Edinburgh.

David Gauld and **Alexander Walker** (see Chapter 3) also

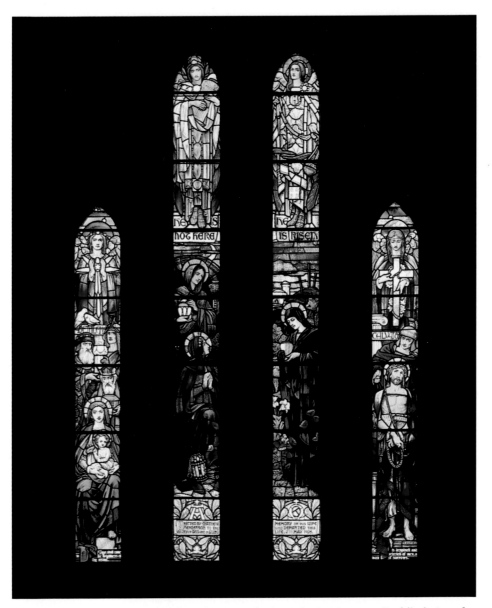

The Henderson Memorial, Stephen Adam and Alf Webster, New Kilpatrick Parish Church, Bearsden, 1910.

designed for Adam on a freelance basis. However Gauld's designs for Adam in Brechin Cathedral are too literal in their execution and lack the subtlety of his best work for Guthrie & Wells, implying a lack of participation by the designer in their execution. By contrast Alexander Walker's figure panels for Adam executed for a church in Leith and now preserved in the Ely Stained-glass Museum are among the best executed examples of his style.

On the evidence of Stephen Adam Junior's surviving independent work, his relationship with his father was close; several commissions, notably his window at **Kilsyth Parish Church**, show a clarity of design and a control of colour which in no way fall below the high standards set by Stephen Adam Senior. However, it was young Stephen's great misfortune to have a serious row with his father which led in 1904 to the destruction of their partnership. For a time young Adam struck up a partnership with Robert Paterson, a skilled cabinet-maker, and together they produced fine furniture in the Glasgow Style operating under the name *The Crafts* around 1905–1909. Stephen Adam Junior's breach with his father was to prove permanent and, bitter at the loss of his inheritance, he emigrated to America where for a time he worked in Hollywood designing glass and furniture for the film studios. He died in 1960.

ALF WEBSTER: FROM TALENT TO GENIUS

Despairing of a reconciliation with his son and deprived of his chief assistant, Stephen Adam Senior succeeded in employing a brilliant young designer, **Alf Webster**. Initially a temporary replacement only, Webster's extraordinary talents as draughtsman, designer and glass stainer within a short while made him utterly indispensable to the older man.

Webster's aptitude for colour was as formidable as Adam's and he was also a portrait painter of exceptional ability, with virtually all his figures being drawn from life studies. These qualities alone would have been enough to have assured him a prominent place among Scottish stained-glass artists, but what lifted him into the category of genius was his capacity to combine all these talents with an unrivalled control of technique.

Christ enters the New Jerusalem *(detail)*, *Alf Webster, Landsdowne Parish Church, Glasgow, 1913.*

The Crucifixion (detail), Alf Webster, south transept window, Lansdowne Parish Church, Glasgow, 1913.

Many fine designers have found the conflict between the concept and the execution of their ideas in glass to be an insurmountable one. Webster, by the age of 28, was producing glass which, for technical control of colour, texture and transparency, alone among his contemporaries, can bear comparison with that other genius of stained glass, the Irish artist **Harry Clarke**.

Webster's early work for Adam appears to have been confined to domestic panels and cartooning. However, by the time of Adam's death in 1910, the younger artist had virtually taken over the studio. For the next four years his prolific, almost volcanic, output of work is compelling evidence not only of great physical and intellectual energy but also an indication of the relief he must have felt in being free from the constraints of working in the house style of the older man. Nevertheless his affection for the older artist was genuine and heartfelt and has been touchingly recorded in the small but very beautiful memorial lancet dedicated to him in the side porch of **New Kilpatrick Parish Church**. Entitled *First Fruits*, this rich, almost exotically coloured panel (opposite) strikes a deeply personal note for the artist not only as a memorial to his dead master but as celebration of his young son and future successor, **Gordon Webster**, who is depicted as an angelic youth.

Webster now replaced Adam's colour schemes with a new and equally rich palette, but one which included a great deal of white glass with aciding, abrasion, plating and faceting of the glass. The painting of the glass is also very distinctive with a broad all-over **stipple** on the faces and limbs of the figures which, while preserving remarkable detail and texture, actually increases the dramatic power and transparency of the glass. The range of windows by Webster at New Kilpatrick Parish Church is probably the most comprehensive including the great west window, where he collaborated with Stephen Adam on the completion of the older artist's final great window, and a series of independent designs over the next few years until his death.

To appreciate the unique quality of Webster's contribution and the enormity of Scotland's loss in his premature death (at the Western Front during the First World War) one must personally visit **Lansdowne Parish Church** in Glasgow, where his great north and south transept windows are among the crowning achievements of Scottish stained glass. Executed just prior to his departure for France, the south transept, with its depiction of Glasgow as the New Jerusalem, overwhelms the viewer by the sheer power of its composition and the intensity of its colour. Then, as each component part of the window is separately examined, the richness of the artist's imaginative powers becomes apparent, as birds, animals and insects emerge from the foliage of the borders like a glorious medieval manuscript.

The Stephen Adam Memorial, Alf Webster, New Kilpatrick Parish Church, Bearsden, 1911.

"WE·BELIEVE·IN·THE·RESURRECTION·OF·THE·DEAD
·AND·THE·LIFE·OF·THE·WORLD·TO·COME"

To·the·glory·o ·God·and·in·loving·memory·of
Frances·Cleugh·who·died· t·Ardrossa· 25ᵗʰ·May·1894·

CHAPTER 3

GLASGOW OF THE 1880s AND 1890s

Beginning with the Great Exhibition of 1851, the role of the international exhibition as a means of stimulating the development of new products and industries became a familiar feature of economic life in western Europe and America. This chapter considers Scotland's share of these extravaganzas, starting with the 1886 exhibition in Edinburgh. The most important exhibitions were both staged in Kelvingrove Park, Glasgow, in 1888 and in 1901. These were international in scope and provided a great stimulus for design in general, and stained glass in particular.

OPPOSITE: Angel plucking tulips *(detail)*, *Harrington Mann, St Andrew's Episcopal Church, Ardrossan, 1894.*

J & W GUTHRIE:
THE GREAT COMMERCIAL STUDIO

Vikings at Largs, Sir James Guthrie, Knockderry Castle, Argyllshire, 1887.

The most important and prolific of the new studios to emerge in Glasgow during the 1880s was that of **John and William Guthrie**, first established as a firm of painters and decorators by their father, John Guthrie Senior, in 1850. Both John and William received their initial training at their father's hands before attending Glasgow School of Art in the early 1870s.

John Guthrie, as a founder member of the Art Workers' Guild, was very much involved in the new direction in the decorative arts epitomised in the **Arts and Crafts movement**. He personally provided a link between these English-based

The Arts and Crafts Movement

The early 1880s were a crucial time for the decorative arts as the wide acceptance of the aesthetic principles pioneered by William Morris, Daniel Cottier, Bruce Talbert and Christopher Dresser inspired new artistic organisations. The Century Guild (1882) and the Art Workers' Guild (1884) were to provide a crucial launching pad and a practical and philosophical foundation for a new direction in the decorative arts, known as the Arts and Crafts movement. Initially stressing hand-crafted manufacture, the ideals of the movement were for unity of function and design, a 'fitness for purpose', where the structural features formed part of the decoration, producing a harmonious whole.

developments and a new art grouping at home known collectively, if somewhat incongruously, as the **Glasgow Boys**.

It originated with a series of small grouping of individual artists who, despite wide differences of style and temperament, began to effect a coalition of sentiment against the academic establishment in historical and genre painting represented by the Royal Society of Arts, and the Glasgow Art Club. All of them were to a greater or lesser degree responsive to, and influenced by, the work of the contemporary Dutch and French artists, painting very much in the open air rather than from memory or sketch in the studio. The natural landscape and figure subjects were profoundly attractive to young artists seeking to break out of what they saw as the academy's rigor mortis.

Daniel Cottier's expanding business interests were also to have a direct bearing on the fortunes of John and William Guthrie. At the end of 1886, Andrew Wells, suffering from overwork and recurrent chest infections, was persuaded by Cottier to abandon his Glasgow business and emigrate to Australia. In Sydney he became a partner, together with Cottier's friend and fellow apprentice John Lamb Lyon, in the firm of Lyon, Cottier & Co, then the leading decorative firm in the colony. Although no documentation exists, there is little doubt that much of Wells's and indeed Cottier's contract work in Scotland now passed to the Guthries. In particular, William Leiper, who had consistently employed both Wells and Cottier in decorating his buildings, now turned increasingly to them for similar works.

In 1887, in an important commission, **Sir James Guthrie**, then leader of the Glasgow Boys was contracted to design two windows for William Leiper's substantial extensions to **Knockderry Castle**, an early Alexander Thomson mansion for the Glasgow carpet manufacturer, James Templeton. The first was a series of four panels

each containing the figure of a single character from Scott's novel *The Heart of Midlothian*. The second consisted of three square top-light panels for a bay window, depicting scenes relating to the Battle of Largs. Executed in a very broad painterly style, these depict King Hakon, the Battle of Largs, and the Vikings dragging their long boats overland to Loch Lomond. Further panels by Guthrie for Leiper's Auchterarder mansion, **Ruthven Towers**, were also designed about this time. Guthrie's stained glass was, however, merely a passing phase in a career as a painter: neither he nor his biographers subsequently refer to it.

What the studio needed was a specialist who

could both design and make stained glass, and at the end of 1887 they acquired one with the return to Glasgow of **Norman McLeod Macdougall**. For 16 years Macdougall had been chief glass painter and latterly a designer in Daniel Cottier's London studio. Macdougall had worked with Cottier on many significant projects, notably at Cairndhu House, Helensburgh (1872), where his name can still be seen, and also in Jedburgh Old Parish Church, where he decorated the chancel.

Macdougall's work for the firm at this time was barely distinguishable from that produced in the Cottier studio and his palette consisted chiefly of deep browns, olive greens, ruby and dark blue, with a liberal use of white glass and silver stain particularly for draperies. By far his best church glass from this early period is the small superbly painted two-light vestibule window in Leiper's **Hyndland Church** (1889). Depicting two angels in the style of **Henry Holiday**, with silvery-white robes and ruby wings, it was given extra care in execution since it was the personal gift of the Guthrie brothers in memory of their late father. Macdougall was of course not the only designer used by the firm in this early period, for, through John Guthrie, the studio had also secured the services of Frederick Vincent Hart, Daniel Cottier's chief freelance designer.

Hart's ability as an all round designer was far greater than Macdougall's, a fact reflected by his independence, and ability to design on request for more than one firm. The first major opportunity for the Guthries to show off their new talent came with the Glasgow International Exhibition of 1888. In the intense competition between the local firms, the Guthries emerged with the lion's share of the stained-glass commissions. Their chief exhibit took the form of large decorative screens divided into rectangular panels, each depicting a different aspect of Women's Industries, designed by Hart. The current location of these panels is unknown.

Following their exhibition success, the studio received many new commissions and in the spring of the following year John Guthrie moved to London, where he set up a new showroom in Oxford Street. It seems fairly certain that Hart's panels from the exhibition were shown in London. They attracted the attention and admiration

Praise, Norman Macleod Macdougall, Hyndland Parish Church, Glasgow, 1889.

OPPOSITE: Vikings at Loch Lomond, *Sir James Guthrie, Knockderry Castle, Argyllshire, 1887.*

The Thanksgiving of Noah, *Christopher Whall, the Clark Memorial Church, Largs, 1889-90. Together with* The Sacrifice of Abraham *this undoubtably represents the most beautiful of Whall's windows for the new Clark Memorial Church. By any standard these are remarkable windows and their rich colouring, balanced composition and extensive use of white glass, were in marked contrast with the equally effective but very different works by Stephen Adam in the same church.*

of **Christopher Whall**, a remarkable designer whose total dedication to the pursuit of personal excellence and control in stained glass would shortly establish him as the most important English artist in the medium since Morris and Burne-Jones.

Like Guthrie, Whall was a founder member of the **Arts and Crafts Society**. It was in their second exhibition in 1898 that his connection with the Glasgow studio was first revealed, when the Guthries exhibited glass to his designs. There followed a series of windows by him for the new Clark Memorial Church in Largs. Sadly, Whall was evidently dissatisfied with the execution of his designs and within a short time he severed his connection with the studio.

Whall's dissatisfaction lay in the realisation that a new and revolutionary breakthrough in glass technology had occurred at the Southwark-based firm of Britten & Gilson. This new glass, manufactured at the suggestion of the architect E S Prior, was of irregular thickness and rich jewel-like translucency, and by the action of acid and chipping could produce a **saturated colour** unobtainable in other glass. Christened '**Prior's Early English**' or 'slab' glass, it was difficult to cut because of its extreme variations of thickness and equally difficult to lead. However its early results were revolutionary and Whall had no option but to switch to Britten & Gilson, who, for a time, retained a monopoly on their discovery.

GUTHRIE COLLABORATORS

William Guthrie continued to recruit craftsmen and designers in Scotland. Among these the most interesting was certainly **William Stewart**. He joined the firm in 1887 and in 1888 was attending evening classes at Glasgow School of Art. His work for the Guthries was of such a high order that within a short time he was made foreman of the Glass Shop, a post he held for almost 20 years. His

domestic leadwork panels, often combining figured white and plain glasses, bevelled or brilliant cut, were highly distinctive and helped to define a commercial house style for the studio. His work was widely used for door panels, top sash windows, and office and saloon screens. Armorial escutcheons, or geometric ornament or formalised plant motifs are the predominant decorative features of his work. However, when the occasion required something extra special, Stewart was more than ready to deliver.

The Dragonfly Window and The Bat Window, William Stewart, Ruthven Towers, Auchterarder, 1888. Two of the three panels, executed in turquoise, blue, lemon, lilac and green opalescent figured glasses, which also featured a lily pond with birds and a night sky with clouds. Inspired by Japanese prints, these panels reveal Stewart as a clever designer and superb craftsman.

The most remarkable work currently attributed to him dates from 1888 and reveals for the first time in Scotland the impact of the new American range of **opalescent glasses** on domestic design. The window was designed as part of a large commission for William Leiper's Auchterarder mansion, Ruthven Towers. This Scots Baronial-style mansion built in 1882–3 had been decorated by Cottier, who supplied glass for the front hall and the main stair window. However following the success of the 1888 Exhibition, Leiper had commissioned the Guthrie studio to supply additional stained-glass panels for the drawing, dining and billiard rooms. For this project in the Guthrie's home town, nothing but the best would suffice and Stewart produced a superlative three-light window.

The year 1889 was in every respect a truly remarkable year for Scottish art and stained glass. For the Guthrie brothers it marked the beginning of their long connection with **David Gauld** and **Harrington Mann**, two of the younger artists on the fringes of the group known as the Glasgow Boys.

The Shepherdess, David Gauld, c. 1889–90 (Private collection, Glasgow).

Gauld, like his friends **Charles Rennie Mackintosh, E A Hornel** and **George Henry,** was profoundly influenced by the linear qualities of **Japanese art**. His superb line drawings for the *Glasgow Weekly Citizen* and his extraordinary painting *St Agnes* show that, though he shared a studio with Harrington Mann, it was the contemporary experiments of Hornel and Henry which had a great impact upon his painting and stained-glass designs for the Guthries. The joint debt of Hornel and Gauld in their contemporary paintings to the exuberant colour schemes of **Adolphe Monticelli** is clear and obvious.

The close relationship between Hornel's painting and Gauld's domestic stained glass, which has hitherto escaped notice, is clearly seen when Hornel's experimental painting of 1898, *The Goatherd,* and Gauld's equally remarkable set of panels for the Guthries depicting shepherdesses are compared. Designed for alterations to a house in Kelvinside by William Leiper, each of Gauld's panels, like Hornel's painting, depicts a long-haired girl seated on the side of a wooded hill tending sheep. In terms of colour they are quite different. However there is a similarity in the linear division of the landscape and the use of the compositional device of the tree to introduce a sense of perspective into this otherwise two-dimensional arrangement, giving both works the same thrust and vitality. This was not the only time that Gauld was to be profoundly moved by Hornel and George Henry's experimental painting.

In the early 1890s Gauld began designing a series of hall windows for the Guthries on the theme of **music and dancing**, depicting tall slender maidens in woodland glades, playing a variety of musical instruments. They are among the most successful of all Gauld's domestic designs, and were clearly the works from which he as an artist derived the most pleasure, displaying in the drawing of the figures the long-limbed languid maidens of the Pre-Raphaelites and the streamlined asymmetry of Japanese art, which are the dominant characteristics of his composition.

Praise (detail), David Gauld, for J & W Guthrie, Upper Largo Parish Church, Fife, 1895.

Youth, *Harrington Mann, for J & W Guthrie, Lambhill Crematorium, Glasgow, c. 1895.*

In his church glass Gauld was much less at ease. Often, as with his Ascension window at Skelmorlie Parish Church (1895), it could be vigorously drawn and boldly coloured. Just as frequently it could be overworked and dry, as in the sequence of windows in Ibrox Parish Church. But at its best, as in his complete scheme for J J Burnett's St Andrews Scots Church in Buenos Aires (1895–*c*.1910), it was boldly drawn, richly coloured, and of equal merit to any of his easel paintings. One only has to compare his fine sequence of dryad portraits of the 1890s with his equally imaginative and serene *Praise* window in **Upper Largo Parish Church** (p.51) to appreciate that by neglecting his designs in glass Gauld has suffered a great injustice at the hands of posterity.

Harrington Mann similarly has left some of his finest work in stained glass. Like Gauld his first reputation came as a painter and decorator when in 1890 he executed a series of mural panels depicting **Women's Industries** for J J Burnet's Gilmour Institute in the Vale of Leven. Mann's work for the studio, though less prolific than Gauld, was perhaps for that very reason more consistently fine. Several designs for mosaic overmantle panels by Mann were published in *Studio* magazine, but their location is unknown. One particularly attractive panel on the theme of the Scottish ballad 'Bessie Bell and Mary Gray,' designed by Mann *c*.1894 for the studio window, is now in the People's Palace collection, Glasgow.

In 1894 Mann designed a very beautiful single-light window for St Andrew's Episcopal Church in **Ardrossan**, executed in a much lighter palette than most of Gauld's works. The main subject is the Crucifixion; however, it is the panel beneath that marks this window out from its contemporaries. It depicts an angel gathering tulips in a wicker basket and is one of the finest examples of the Glasgow Style in ecclesiastical glass (Chapter frontispiece).

Another three-light window by Mann for the Chapel of **Lambhill Crematorium**, Glasgow, largely executed in white glass, embodies the visual pun of the *Ages of Mann*. Other glass by Mann from this period can be seen at Liff Parish Church near Dundee, and at J J Burnet's Corrie Parish Church in Arran. A richly decorative two-light window of the *Good Samaritan* (1892), formerly in Trinity

Clairmont Parish Church, Glasgow (now the Henry Wood Hall), is in the permanent collection of the Ely Stained-glass Museum. Mann's largest work in stained glass was probably his rose window for J J Burnet's St Andrew's Scots Church in Buenos Aires. After 1900 he concentrated on a profitable but artistically impoverished career as a fashionable portrait painter in London.

It was also in 1896 that John Guthrie first acquired the services of the graphic designer and muralist **Robert Anning Bell**. Bell's reputation as an artist was already very high due to extensive exposure in the pages of *Studio* in 1893, where his remarkable designs for bookplates were regularly featured. Guthrie required a special set of designs for the studio's tender for the chancel windows of the new royal church at Crathie. Bell duly produced a series of sketches for five single lancets featuring Christ flanked by St Andrew, St Columba, St Margaret and St Bridget.

It is I, be not afraid,
Robert Anning Bell for J & W Guthrie, Partick Old Parish Church, Glasgow, 1896.

In later years, while lecturing at the Royal College in London, Bell would modestly recount how Willie Stewart and his skilled craftsmen helped the novice designer to modify his cartoons, teaching him by example how to integrate his leadwork and harmonise his colours. The several versions of his designs for these windows are now in the People's Palace collection. The completed windows were installed in 1895 and the following year a two-light window for Partick Old Parish Church, Glasgow, also designed by Bell demonstrated just how quickly this remarkable designer learned his craft.

Of the many schemes executed by him for the studio, his complete scheme for the Alexander Elder Chapel of the Western Infirmary (1926), and the Nurses' Chapel of the Royal Infirmary (1912), both in Glasgow, are the most easily accessible.

GUTHRIE RIVALS

William Meikle & Sons

One of the chief rivals to the Guthries was the firm of **William Meikle & Sons**. Founded in 1838, in part of the 18th-century premises of the old Glasgow Bottleworks, the firm had already enjoyed 48 years of uninterrupted trade when in 1886 they diversified into the field of glass staining.

In 1888, when overall management had passed from its aging founder to his son, **William T Meikle**, the first stained glass attributable to the firm was executed for a display by Alexander Gardiner and Sons, a leading firm of cabinet-makers for their exhibit at the Glasgow International Exhibition of that year. The Exhibition presented a crucial opportunity to the firm. Only a handful of William Meikle's own sketch designs have survived but on the evidence of the earliest surviving ecclesiastical commission (in the Ramshorn Church, Ingram Street, Glasgow) it is certain that he obtained his training as a glass stainer and cartoonist with Stephen Adam. Significantly all of Meikle's work of the 1880s, like Adam's, suffered to a greater or lesser degree from deterioration of paint work. Indeed, it may be that, being trained by Adam, Meikle shared his formulas and hence his technical difficulties.

Meikle could not emulate Adam's stylistic leaps but seems to have accepted his own limitations and set out to secure the best available design talent while retaining full control of the management of the studio. In 1892 he successfully recruited the first of two young, highly talented designers from the Decorative Studio of the Dumbarton ship builder William Denny & Co. The first, **Jonathan C Carr**, was a Dumbarton man. He was already a skilled craftsman, and chief assistant to the Foreman of the Decorative Department. Carr's versatility as an all-round designer of general furnishings and metalwork was a vital asset for Meikle in his efforts to obtain a toe-hold in the lucrative field of ship decoration. For this reason he also appears to have tried to recruit his boss, **John Tytler Stewart**. Born in Leslie, Fife, in 1858, Stewart, the son of a merchant draper, was apprenticed at 13 to a local firm of decorators and, on the completion of his time

Charity, William Meikle Junior, the Ramshorn Church, Ingram Street, 1887 (now Strathclyde University Theatre).

in 1877, secured a job with a Glasgow decorating firm and began attending night classes at Glasgow School of Art.

He worked for a while in London before returning to Glasgow in 1881. After two attempts to survive as an independent studio in 1895 he swallowed his pride and became a full-time employee of William Meikle and Sons. In 1896 Stewart and J C Carr held a joint exhibition of their work in Meikle's showroom, which attracted much attention.

Almost immediately the firm achieved its first national publicity when the new magazine *The Artist* devoted five pages to a review of the show. The reviewer lavished praise on Meikle for awarding such public recognition to their designers. The Glasgow magazine *Quiz* was even more enthusiastic, publishing a review under the heady title 'New Art Movement in Glasgow'.

The partnership came to an end when Carr moved south to Manchester, but Stewart remained as Meikle's principal designer and acquired a new collaborator and assistant in John Stark Melville. Melville had joined the firm as an apprentice and had spent some time working as an improver with Christopher Whall before returning to the firm in about 1898. Stewart was also assisted by his son and apprentice Charles Edward Stewart. Stewart and Melville together experimented on various methods of protecting their glass staining from decay before developing a complex technique derived from the embossing side of the firm using a combination of abrasion, and etching with hydrofluoric acid. By this method the essential repeat patterns on costume and crucial details such as the hands and faces of figures were created while traditional glass painting was virtually eliminated.

Autumn, J T Stewart, for William Meikle & Sons, Dowanhill, Glasgow, c.1900.

Glasgow Style in place: door and window panels in the Dowanhill area of Glasgow, fine glass in an accessible domestic setting.

Their first window by this technique was a memorial window for Queen Victoria in Bo'ness Parish Church installed in 1903. The following year Meikle and Sons announced the technique to the glass trade as the 'Cameo Process' and began claiming exclusive rights. Such a claim was rash in a profession already noted for its technical innovation. **Oscar Paterson** among others had been experimenting with hydrofluoric acid, plating and other techniques since at least 1896 and probably earlier.

The effect of the '**Cameo Glass**' is impressive. A window in this process by Stewart and his son Charles for Partick Old Parish Church, Glasgow, is on display in the Museum of Religion, Glasgow, where it can be seen at close quarters.

Among the most interesting work carried out by the studio were Stewart's domestic designs for the new housing in the Dowanhill area of Glasgow, where Meikle and Sons secured a large contract which included several thousand panels of domestic glass, consisting chiefly of door, transom and half-light panels in pure glass mosaic. The subjects are mainly formalised floral motifs in the distinctive streamlined style now known as the Glasgow Style.

Many other studios made a contribution both to the origin and spread of this style, but none were more voluminous in their output than Meikle's. By far their most prolific designer in this style was the young **Andrew Rigby Gray**. An Edinburgh man, Gray studied at the Royal College of Art, London, returned to Edinburgh in 1904, and joined Meikle. It is ironic that some of the finest so called 'Glasgow Style' designs were conceived in Edinburgh, where Gray continued to live for the next 16 years.

After 1907, when J T Stewart and his son Charles left to form their own studio, Rigby Gray became the chief designer, a post held until the collapse of Meikle's in the depression of the 1930s. Work was difficult to find; Gray moved to Polmont, where he continued to design on a freelance basis, chiefly for J P McPhie & Co., who had purchased most of Meikle's glass stock and plant. He also freelanced for the Abbey Studio, the stained-glass department of the **City Glass Company** in Edinburgh.

Crossing the Bar,
J T & C E Stewart,
Leslie Street Church of
Scotland, Glasgow,
Pollokshields Destroyed
by fire, 1985.

CHAPTER 4

THE TURN OF THE CENTURY

THE CREATION OF THE GLASGOW STYLE

In this chapter we look at key movers in the making of the Glasgow Style, led by Fra Newbery and Oscar Paterson.

There were many factors which contributed to the explosion of talent in the field of interior decoration in Glasgow during the 1890s. The city was at the height of its industrial power; it had a large and growing middle class with surplus income to spend on lavish new houses and mansions. The surplus income came from a huge colonial empire providing a captive market for goods of all kinds. However the demand for better quality of production and design came from a generation raised on the writings of **John Ruskin** and **William Morris**. The revolution in practice began in the art schools and in Glasgow that revolution is synonymous with the name of **Fra Newbery**.

FRA NEWBERY:
NEW DIRECTIONS IN ART TRAINING

As the energetic Director of Glasgow School of Art, Francis, 'Fra', Newbery made a great personal contribution to developing the burgeoning talent in interior decoration and design in Glasgow at the turn of the century. He received his early art training at Bridport School of Art in Dorset, then continued first as a student and student teacher at the National Art Training School at South Kensington, London.

Although a personal friend and champion of the 'Glasgow Boys', Newbery was acutely aware of the limitations of their base of patronage. Even for the most talented of this group (and their slightly later contemporaries associated with Patrick Geddes of Edinburgh) the struggle to establish a regular and critically sympathetic clientele was an uphill one. Newbery recognised that in a country like

OPPOSITE: Gather Ye the Rosebuds, *E A Taylor*, for Lord Weir of Cathcart, 1902. Less stylised than the contemporary works of people like Charles Rennie Mackintosh and Herbert MacNair, this panel depicts two young girls in a woodland setting executed in a manner heavily influenced by Oscar Paterson. Taylor received further commissions about this time that for ingle-neuk cabinets and a frieze from Hugh McCulloch for the music room at his house 'Hughenden' where they complemented slightly earlier windows by David Gauld, variants on the latter's 1891 Music *series.*

Art training at the turn of the century

Prior to Newbery's arrival, Glasgow, like other art schools throughout Britain, was required to follow a 'National Course of Instruction' and submit its results to the Government Department of Science and Art at South Kensington. The course consisted of a series of stages beginning with elementary drawing, shading, painting, figure drawing, geometrical drawing, perspective, modelling and, as a unifying discipline, the general principles of design as applied to manufactures. Most students were part-timers being in daytime employment and attended either in the early morning or at evening classes. The day classes were mainly the preserve of the daughters of the middle classes who were taught drawing as an 'accomplishment', and not for career purposes.

Scotland the odds against two distinctive schools of painting surviving in close proximity were extremely high. The opportunity for a third was simply non-existent. On the other hand the sheer complexity of **Glasgow's manufacturing base** under the umbrella of the heavy industries of shipbuilding, marine engineering and locomotive construction presented a constant demand for good design. The city's numerous brass and iron foundries, cabinet-making, textile, pottery and glass industries were sound sources of future employment and its was in line with their needs that Newbery began to develop the teaching capacities of Glasgow School of Art.

It was that archetypal 'Glasgow Girl' **Jessie Rowat**, the future Mrs Newbery, who was the first of his students to demonstrate an interest in stained glass. Jessie was the daughter of William Rowat, a wealthy tea importer. Although her chief interest as a student and subsequently as a member of staff was embroidery, her early interest in stained glass led her to design a panel *Tempestas* in 1889, which won a bronze medal in the national competition at South Kensington.

In 1890 the second successful entry in the national competition served to underline the deficiencies in the School's facilities. The distinguished judges, led by William Morris, while awarding a bronze medal to **Victoria M Carruthers** for 'a remarkably charming and poetic design' were concerned to note that 'the execution is quite unworthy of it and ill-adapted to stained glass'. Armed with this critical evidence, Newbery by 1893 had persuaded the Governors of the necessity of establishing a technical workshop, staffed by qualified instructors. In his annual report he proudly announced the setting up of the workshop:

The Stained Glass Studio, Glasgow School of Art, c. 1911.

This room has been specially fitted up, and artist craftsmen have been engaged to give instruction in such subjects as Glass Staining, Pottery, Repoussé and Metal Work, Wood Carving and Book Binding, besides Artistic Needlework taught by a lady.

The working conditions for those attempting to pursue so many mutually incompatible activities in one room must have been primitive indeed. However the list of students who immediately benefited from its cramped provisions is impressive and included two night students, **Charles Rennie Mackintosh** and **Herbert Macnair**, and two gifted day students, **Frances** and **Margaret MacDonald**. Newbery actively encouraged them to work together.

The first choice by Newbery for the important post of artist craftsman in stained glass was Norman McLeod Macdougall, the veteran glass painter from Cottier & Co who had returned to Glasgow in 1887 and was now designing for J & W Guthrie. Although he continued to support the School in many ways, Macdougall's time on the staff was short-lived and by the following year he had quit to establish his own studio. He probably had a hand in selecting his successors, Harry Roe and William Stewart, who both worked for J & W Guthrie. Stewart in particular was a first-rate craftsman and designer and, apart from his role as foreman of the glass department at Guthrie's, he was also responsible for some of their best domestic leaded glass designs.

The Editor's Room window, *Charles Rennie Mackintosh (executed by William Stewart), Glasgow Herald Building, 1894. One of the panels from this period which, in their flowing organic shapes, illustrate the rapidly developing decorative brilliance of Mackintosh, whilst equally betraying the strong technical influence of William Stewart.*

Thistle, J Herbert McNair, Barrhead, c. 1900 (private collection).

The benefits of Newbery's innovation were seen in the form of some exciting designs for stained glass. The best known are Margaret MacDonald's two designs *The Path of Life* (1893) and *Summer* (1894), which won recognition as prizewinning exhibits by the outside assessor, Stephen Adam. This was followed in 1894 by Charles Rennie Mackintosh's earliest designs for stained glass at the Glasgow Herald Building, Craigie Hall, Bellahouston, and in the still unlocated 'Library for a House' in Glasgow. This latter commission, designed on a freelance basis for J & W Guthrie, for the first time featured a fully integrated scheme incorporating furnishings, stencil work, metalwork and stained glass.

A stained-glass panel *c.* 1896 by Herbert Macnair, reproduced in the *Studio*, shows a similar debt to Stewart in its confident use of clear glass and leadwork which could never have been achieved without a thorough grounding in sound technique. Though neither Mackintosh nor McNair executed their own glass (both relied on J & W Guthrie and McCulloch & Co), their designs show a good understanding of the medium. A decorative screen designed for the

The Water Sprite, W G Morton, 1896 (Glasgow Museums: The People's Palace). Though Morton was responsible for the design, the execution was almost certainly by William Stewart and compares favourably with the bat window (p. 49) at Auchterarder (1883). As a piece of stained glass it is a triumphant affirmation of the best qualities of the Glasgow Style. The integration of subject and leadlines is total, the painting is confined to the absolute minimum, while the ripples and textures of the glass are skilfully manipulated to wonderful effect.

School of Art's entry to the 1902 Turin Exhibition is typical of Macnair's approach. Its subject matter, two identical reversed images of a long-haired girl in a bower of flowers, reveals the unmistakable influence of his wife Frances and her sister Margaret.

William Gibson Morton, who was better known for work in other media, specialised in general interior decoration, stencil work and sign writing. He was also a landscape artist in oils and watercolour. He attended the School from 1891 to 1895 and was recruited by Newbery to the staff of the Design Department in 1897. As a designer of glass he freelanced for many firms, including Oscar Paterson, John C Hall and McCulloch & Co. In the 1920s and 1930s he was also to be responsible for the decoration of a series of restaurants for the City Bakery Co and the cafeteria of Green's Playhouse (latterly the Apollo Centre), all in Glasgow. One of his finest works dating from 1895 is *The Water Sprite*, now in the People's Palace collection.

Among other students who produced designs for stained glass during the 1890s were Emily Hutcheson, Dorothy Carleton Smyth, Monro S Orr, Stephen Adam Junior, W J Tonner, Henry T Wyse, Jessie M McGeehan, De Courcey Lewthwaite Dewar, John C Hall and W M Petrie. Of this group only the work of Smyth, Adam and Hall are currently identified. Of the latter three only Adam and Hall chose glass as their chief medium.

Dorothy Carleton Smyth began her art training in Manchester before switching to Glasgow School of Art in 1898. A versatile artist, equally at home in oil and watercolour, she specialised in book illustration and costume design. In her second year she produced a stained-glass panel based on the legend of Tristan and Isolde which earned her a place on the staff of the School. In 1933 she was appointed Director of the School but her sudden death robbed her of the chance to fulfil the opportunity.

SOLDE·MARH·S·UINEH·UHO·QAVE THE·LOVE·POTION·TO·TRISTAN

Isolde, *Dorothy Carleton Smyth, Glasgow School of Art, 1901 (reproduced by kind permission of Glasgow School of Art). This panel which earned Dorothy a place on the staff of the Glasgow School of Art was included in the School's entry for 1901 International Exhibition, then in the School's entry at Turin in 1902 and remains on display in the School to the present day.*

Peace be Still,
*Alexander Walker for
McCulloch & Co, St
Michael's Episcopal
Church, Helensburgh, c.
1896.*

In 1898 William Stewart retired and was replaced by a young craftsman, **Alexander Walker** who had obtained his art training at the Glasgow Athenaeum. In 1896, his design for a stained-glass window secured a silver medal at South Kensington and he was recruited by **Hugh McCulloch**, one of the Athenaeum's Governors, to provide designs to supplement the work of his other freelance designers, David Gauld and Harrington Mann. Through his appointment to the staff of the School of Art, Walker not only widened his connections but began freelancing for many other studios. The increasing burden of his busy career led him in 1902 to temporarily relinquish his post. In the late 1920s he moved to Kirkwall in Orkney, where he supervised and designed many of the new windows being installed in St Magnus Cathedral by Oscar Paterson. He died there in 1927.

Fishers of Men,
*Alexander Walker for
McCulloch & Co, St
James Parish Church,
Pollock, Glasgow, 1895.*

EXPONENTS OF THE GLASGOW STYLE

McCulloch and Company

One of the smaller firms of the 1880s in Glasgow which sought to rival both J & W Guthrie and Cottier & Co was that established by **Hugh McCulloch**, a former employee of Daniel Cottier.

In 1883 he decided to diversify into stained-glass production. This involved him in a new partnership with **Charles Gow**, a former apprentice of John Cairney, who had been employed as a glass painter and cartoonist with Daniel Cottier since 1866. The discovery of a large stair window by this partnership in a house in Leadcameroch, Milngavie (c.1883–5), reveals a heavy dependence on the studio style of Cottier.

McCulloch & Gow's earliest surviving church glass is the three-light window by Gow for New Kilpatrick Parish Church, Bearsden. The subject depicts three different aspects of the parable of *The Good Samaritan*. It reveals Gow as a confident draughtsman, and his glass-staining is light and effective. One of their most important jobs of the late 1880s was the decoration for the newly built Clifton House, the Pollokshields mansion of William Costigane, owner of Glasgow's Bonanza Warehouse. For this scheme Gow produced a splendid hall window on the subject of the Trojan War.

Wisdom, *James Adam for McCulloch & Gow, c. 1883 (Private collection, Bearsden). As in the great stair window at Cairndhu, the window is effectively a large screen of variegated quarries into which are inserted four figure panels.*
BELOW: Helen & Paris, *Charles Gow, Pollokshields, Glasgow, c. 1889 (private collection). The treatment of the main subject in this panel is similar to Cottier's, but the supporting framework of shimmering, silvery-toned floral borders, pilasters, and chubby cherubim is very different.*

Music, *David Gauld for McCulloch & Co, c. 1890-91 (private collection).*

In 1891 recurrent chest infections forced Gow to emigrate to Australia to work once again for Daniel Cottier. McCulloch turned for design assistance to the talented duo David Gauld and Harrington Mann, who were already working for the Guthries. Gauld's work for these two firms is so close in style and date that it is difficult to separate them, except in one vital aspect. Where Gauld's work for the Guthries ranged from a detailed pictorial style to the sparse, streamlined Japanese-influenced designs like *The Shepherdess*, for McCulloch only the latter style would suffice. His main contribution to the studio's design pool was a series of eight panels depicting young maidens playing a variety of musical instruments. First installed in the music room of a house in Pollokshields, one panel from this series was gifted by the current owner of the firm to the People's Palace.

By 1901 the new style of design identified with the work of the Mackintoshes and McNairs, George Walton and Oscar Paterson was given a further boost by the emergence of a new group of interior designers associated with the leading Glasgow furnishing firm, **Wylie & Lochead**. They had dominated the displays of the 1888 Exhibition and had no intention of relinquishing their crown to rival houses in the Glasgow International Exhibition of 1901. Chief of these new designers were **E A Taylor, John Ednie** and **George Logan**. Taylor, a Greenock man, had joined the firm in 1893 and by 1901 had emerged as their most extrovert interior designer. Ednie had trained as an architect at Edinburgh College of Art before joining the firm in 1898. George Logan, a young designer from Greenock, completed a trio who were to be the firm's secret weapon in the style wars which beckoned with the approaching International Exhibition.

Less original than Mackintosh and his group, these designers formed a commercial bridge between their one-off exclusive creations and the demands of mass production. Their suite of rooms formed the centrepiece of the company's exhibit and for the first time provided a range of reproducible designs for domestic furniture, textiles, carpets, metalwork and stained glass aimed at Scotland's burgeoning upper middle class. The stained glass, which provided a crucial element in these displays, was subcontracted to McCulloch & Co, who as a result benefited by the additional business generated by the success of the show. McCulloch's own special contribution to the 1901 Exhibition was a large historical work by either David Gauld or Harrington Mann depicting *The Coronation of King Robert the Bruce* at Scone.

In 1902 in one of the many spin-off commissions, Taylor redesigned the interior of a late Victorian house in Glencairn Drive, Pollokshields for Lord Weir of Cathcart. The scheme includes a stair window on the theme *Gather ye the Rosebuds* (frontispiece this chapter) which is probably the largest work in opalescent glass made in Scotland. Taylor did not make his own glass, but supplied sketch designs and cartoons which were carried out by McCulloch's craftsmen.

Other commissions followed for John Ednie, who carried out the remodelling of a house in Huntly Gardens, Hillhead, for which he produced some striking top-lights in the style of **Baillie Scott** of stylised trees and birds. The sensation produced by these and other works carried out by the firm persuaded Mackintosh to switch from Guthrie & Wells to McCulloch when in 1903 he designed his most famous work, the Room De Luxe of the **Willow Tearooms**. This jewel-like room with its continuous frieze of opaque white and purple enamelled plant motifs against a background of mirror glass and its 'Cat Doors' created a sensation in contemporary decorative arts. McCulloch's were to continue designing and executing glass commissions until the death of its founder in 1925 but this was to be their finest hour and the high watermark of Mackintosh's achievement in glass. After 1904 Glasgow's brief flirtation with the avant-garde was already beginning to cool.

The Water Mill, *E A Taylor, McCulloch & Co, c. 1902, (private collection, Giffnock).*

THE EPITOME OF GLASGOW STYLE:
OSCAR PATERSON & CO

Although J & W Guthrie operated the most prolific studio of the 1890s, followed closely by Meikle & Sons and McCulloch & Co, they were – in terms of publicity and contemporary critical acclaim – largely eclipsed by the smaller firm established in 1898 by **Oscar Paterson**, who was born in Gorbals in 1863. He appears to have been educated in London, possibly working at Powells of Whitefriars. Alone among his contemporaries, for a time he manufactured his own raw materials, being a fully trained glassmaker and a tutor in glass technology at Gresham College in the 1880s.

In 1889 he opened his first studio in West Regent Street, where he continued to combine the roles of tutor and glass stainer. At a time when most studios were content to keep the individual contributions of their various designers hidden under the studio logo, Paterson, like Meikle, was noted for his acknowledgement of the work of his various assistants and collaborators. Although Paterson and his partner **Harry Thomson** executed many church windows during the 1890s it was their domestic designs which gave them a distinctive edge and first brought their work to international attention in 1898 when the art magazine *Studio* devoted space to their work.

Paterson was fully conversant with new developments in American glass pioneered by **John La Farge** and **Louis Comfort Tiffany**, and sensitive to the problems arising from industrial pollution and under-firing, which had bedevilled the work of artists like Stephen Adam. He experimented in etching on the surface of the glass with hydrofluoric acid as a substitute for key portions of

The Quaint Village, *Oscar Paterson, Bute Gardens, c. 1890 (Glasgow University collection).*

painter work such as hands and faces. The creative exchange of ideas between the various Glasgow studios was not always an amicable affair, and personal rivalries sometimes soured relationships. In 1904 he was unjustly accused of stealing Meikle's Cameo Process. Paterson's contribution to the pool of ideas, however, always greatly outweighed his borrowings.

If the art of Japan was the dominant influence on his approach to the composition of his domestic windows it was the irresistible quaintness of the European (especially German) **folk tale**, which often provided their subject matter. Paterson's minimal use of glass paint and emphasis on the role of the leadlines in defining the chief outlines of the composition led in the direction of pure glass mosaic, which by 1900 had become the dominant characteristic of the Glasgow Style. His influence upon contemporaries like Mackintosh and Walton must have been considerable. Through his prolific output

Galleon, Oscar Paterson, Hillhead, Glasgow, c. 1899 (private collection).

and the widespread coverage given to his work by *Studio*, and slightly later by *Dekorativ Kunst*, it is his impact upon younger designers like E A Taylor, **Jessie M King** and John Ednie which is most obvious.

It should not be thought that Paterson was in any way afraid of strong colour and where the situation demanded it his work could be every bit as powerful as any of his Glasgow contemporaries. This is particularly evident in the years 1900–1920 when, surrounded by a group of young design assistants, he established himself as the favourite designer for several important architectural firms. His small but brilliantly colourful seascape panel for James Salmon Junior's Hat Rack Building in West Regent Street (1902) is typical of his versatility in both colour and materials.

Paterson's longest serving assistant was **John Stark Melville**. He attended Glasgow School of Art in 1881, when he is listed as a glass painter. He worked for J T Stewart and Meikle, whom he quit to join Paterson's studio. His skills as a craftsman were already acknowledged and he was fully appraised of Stewart's Cameo Process. The resulting row which erupted in the

The Sheaves of Barley, *John Bowie for Oscar Paterson, c. 1906 (private collection, Kelvinside, Glasgow).*

press, in which Meikle unjustly accused Paterson of poaching their inventions, was understandable, but Paterson was the antitheses of the kind of hard-headed businessman who indulges in industrial espionage (as his family had cause to lament).

Some of his finest small panels belong to this period, particularly those in a technique which he named '**Ivorine**', whereby a sheet of fluorescent glass flashed on one or both sides is then processed with hydrofluoric acid to etch out the main lines of a composition, and further excavated by means of engraving, cutting and finishing with the lapidiary wheel. The resulting sculptured effect when seen through transmitted light was remarkable.

Melville became Paterson's chief assistant, and a full partner in 1911. His works for Paterson included a good deal of decorative glass for the ill-fated liner the *Lusitania*, and a large memorial window for the First Battalion of the Seaforth Highlanders for a church in Rawalpindi, Pakistan. They alternately designed or executed each other's windows. Melville's connection with the studio lasted nine years. He then emigrated to

Gang East Gang West Hame's Best, *Oscar Paterson, c. 1900 (private collection, Giffnock, Glasgow).*

America, where in 1913 he joined Tiffany & Co. It was his expertise – acquired with Stewart and improved with Paterson – in etching glass in hydrofluoric acid, a skill then unknown in America, which gained him an easy entré to Tiffany: his first job was a window executed entirely in this technique.

By this time Paterson's studio was producing substantial amounts of glass for the Pacific and Oriental Shipping Company among others and a fine ship's saloon, complete with glass, can be seen at the Woodside Hotel, Aberdour, Fife, salvaged from the breaker's yard at Burntisland. Part of Paterson's success lay in the **abandonment of pigment** which had always suffered from salt exposure, and the adoption of special lead calms cored with steel to resist damage by the vibration of the ships' engines. This capacity for adapting his techniques to suit hostile environments was no doubt a key factor in Paterson's securing of the contract for all the glass associated with **Walter McFarlane's** cast-iron Durbar Hall, at Quetta in India. This commission secured his reputation with the Indian Imperial authorities and led to many other contracts.

The Sail on the Horizon, Oscar Paterson, c. 1900 (Glasgow University Collection).

After a lean time during the First World War, Paterson's business began to pick up again but the market for domestic stained glass had withered away during the years of tragedy and austerity. The fairy-tale subject matter of his favourite designs were now significantly out of step with the more strident themes of the **jazz age**. A substantial late commission to provide a complete scheme of stained glass for the restoration of St Magnus' Cathedral, Kirkwall, kept the ecclesiastical side of the studio going throughout the 1920s. In the design, execution and installation of this scheme, Paterson was assisted by Alex Walker, but as the first chill of the Great Depression began to bite the work gradually dried up.

In 1931 he closed the studio but continued to advertise himself as an Artist in Stained Glass from his house. He died 7 November 1934; there were no fulsome obituaries, as there had been the previous year for Robert Anning Bell. He was buried in the Glasgow Necropolis, where his grave remains unmarked.

Small, frail-looking, and deformed by a prominent hunchback, Paterson, dressed in an artist's smock and a corduroy jacket, with his long shoulder-length hair, must have been the butt of much verbal cruelty during his career but his strength of character and astonishing artistic and technical ability enabled him to dominate his chosen profession and command respect and admiration from some of its finest craftsmen.

GEORGE WALTON & CO

The company began in the early 1890s when Miss Catherine Cranston, preparing for the launch of her second tearoom, discovered a new and gifted interior designer in **George Walton**. After employing him to decorate a small snug in her **Argyle Street Tearooms**, Cranston was so impressed by his work that she placed him in charge of the interior design of her new building, under construction in Buchanan Street. Opened in 1896 the furbishment of this remarkable suite of tea, coffee, reading and billiards rooms

Virgo *(detail), George Walton, Carlybank House, Barrhead,* home of Catherine Cranston, c. *1890.*

launched a new movement in Scottish interior decoration and marked the first collaboration between its talented young designer and the architect Charles Rennie Mackintosh.

It was in 1899 that Walton's stained glass caught up with his furnishing designs in the scheme for the redevelopment and extension of the Argyle Street Tearooms. This involved not only the inclusion of substantial glass mosaics, but also a wide range of decorative glass and copper for door panels and furniture inserts. This combination of glass and copper was for a time unique to Walton but was copied by his rivals, including Meikle. At the same time Walton was executing full schemes of church decoration; of note is the Coats Memorial Church in Paisley.

One of his earliest and most successful windows was for Sir William Burrell's House in Devonshire Gardens (1892), Glasgow, on the theme *Gather ye the Rosebuds*. Walton later moved to York, where at the Elm Bank Hotel his glass, tiles, mosaics and furnishings of 1900 are still virtually intact and well worth a pilgrimage.

Copper and glass door panel, George Walton, c.1898 (private collection, Glasgow).

Gather ye the Rosebuds, *George Walton, the Burrell House, Devonshire Gardens, Kelvinside, Glasgow, 1892.*

HERE AM I. SEND ME

THE LORD IS WITH THEE

THOU MIGHTY MAN OF VALOUR

RABBONI

THESE TWELVE JESUS SENT FORTH

THEY STRAIGHTWAY LEFT THEIR NETS & FOLLOWED HIM.

CHAPTER 5

POST-WAR BLUES AND EMPIRE EXHIBITION

After the catastrophic Wall Street crash of 1929 the economy of the developed world went into free fall. Shipbuilding on the Clyde had already begun its slow but remorseless decline due to competition, lack of investment and the shrinkage of imperial markets. All this had its impact on the market for luxury products in Scotland. The resources for high-class decoration in both churches and the private mansions of the rich began to evaporate. In this chapter we look at how stained-glass production survived the onslaught of the Depression, albeit with some notable casualties.

For a time new architectural forms inspired by mass public entertainment such as cinema and dancing provided fresh outlets for decoration and a temporary buffer against the decline of the domestic market. But **Art Deco**, the style most closely associated with these developments, demanded new forms and it was the less expensive and more streamlined medium of embossed glass which flourished during this period. By the early 1930s shipbuilding was at a virtual standstill, symbolised by the stoppage of work on the Cunard Liner 534 (the *Queen Mary*). Studios like William Meikle's and Oscar Paterson's, which had derived a substantial part of their income from domestic work, were in serious trouble and by the middle of the decade had closed their doors forever.

This was the uncertain climate in which a new generation of designers, disciples of the Arts and Crafts tradition, trained principally at Glasgow and Edinburgh Schools of Art, struggled to create their finest work. The dominance of the symbolist/expressionist tendencies in Scottish stained glass of the first half of the 20th

OPPOSITE: *War Memorial window, Margaret Chilton/John Blyth, Bearsden South Parish Church, Glasgow, 1957.*

century can be attributed to the teaching of these two important schools. The influence of **Art Nouveau** in its uniquely Scottish form, the **Glasgow Style**, did not survive the Great War.

GLASGOW IN THE JAZZ AGE

In Glasgow **Robert Anning Bell**, Head of Design at Glasgow School of Art, exerted a powerful influence on all his students and contemporaries. Through his stained-glass designs for Guthrie & Wells and Lowndes & Dury (the London studio established by Christopher Whall's disciples) he also provided a close link to the veteran designer Henry Holiday. This emphasis was if anything strengthened by the departure of Alex Walker and his replacement as stained-glass tutor by **Margaret Chilton**.

Chilton was born in Bristol in 1875, and attended the Royal College of Art in London around 1902, where her tutors were Christopher Whall and Alfred J Drury. In 1906 she had returned to Bristol, where she established her own studio, her earliest window (1907) being in Pilton Church, Somerset. The extent of Chilton's commitment to the credo of the Arts and Crafts movement can be gauged by her description of her working methods recorded in 1924:

> *My aim is to keep the glass clear, to use light and bright colours with a good deal of light background . . . As far as I can, I aim at drawing a good type of person to suggest something above the everyday figure. I would like to make a heroic type to attract children and young people and at the same time keep to the limitations of glass. In our workshop we use only antique and slab glasses (no sheet or other mechanically made glasses). We cast our own leads. I try to make each part of the work good, as I believe that even the cutline should be beautiful in line, for well-planned leadwork is an attraction outside the building. I do not leave anything to an assistant: I make the design, and draw out the cartoon to the last detail, plan bars and divisions, choose and cut the glass. This last is the most important of all because it is impossible for two people to see colour alike, and if the designer cuts his own glass he puts something of himself into it.*

In 1918 Chilton moved to Glasgow, where she was employed briefly on a full-time basis by the City Glass Company, a large commercial glazing firm established in 1903 by **J Marcus McLundie**. Chilton had been employed as a designer craftsman by the firm's stained-glass department, known as the 'Abbey Studio'. However by 1921 she had severed her links with the studio and was employed on a part-time basis as a stained-glass instructor at Glasgow School of Art. In 1922 she established her second studio in Edinburgh in partnership with her former student, **Marjorie Kemp**, and thereafter enjoyed a long and prolific career which lasted until her death in 1962.

Her place as instructor in stained glass was filled again on a part time basis by **Alexander Strachan**, who, for the first time, linked the stained-glass courses at Glasgow and Edinburgh.

GUTHRIE AND WELLS UNLIMITED

In 1899 the return of **Andrew Wells** to Glasgow threatened to create serious competition for J & W Guthrie. However the situation was resolved when John Guthrie retired to pursue a solo career and Wells and his son Archibald became partners in a new public company of Guthrie & Wells. With much new investment this largest of Scottish studios continued to buck the trend by commissioning freelance designers whose cartoons were often executed in part or entirely at the discretion of their skilled glass workers.

Presentation in the Temple, *Robert Burns for Chilton & Kemp, Broughton/St Mary's Church, Edinburgh, 1924.*

Anning Bell had of course introduced a new range of glasses into their studio. However, his design and teaching commitments gradually restricted his work for the studio until in 1920 it became necessary for the company to appoint a full-time designer to take up the general management of the glass workshop. On 12 May they acquired the services of **Charles Paine**, a talented English designer who had recently joined

The Gondola, *Charles Paine, Guthrie & Wells. Cadoro Building, Glasgow, 1921.*

The Harvest Window *(detail), Charles Paine, c. 1922 (City of Glasgow Friendly Society).*

the staff of Edinburgh College of Art as Head of Design. Paine had trained at the Royal College in London under Christopher Whall and **Karl Parsons**.

Like Anning Bell his roots were firmly in the Arts and Crafts movement. His palette is light with blues predominating and, like Chilton, he regularly uses backgrounds of silvery-white slab glass. It is not clear whether he actually executed his own glass in Glasgow. Certainly the terms of his contract imply that the company expected

The Angel of Peace *(detail), Charles Lamb Davidson, Lambhill Crematorium, Glasgow,*

him to concentrate primarily on the production of sketch designs and cartoons. His stay at Guthrie & Wells was short but his impact upon the firm was a healthy one: new catalogues were issued and prominent advertisements placed in *Country Life* and *The Scottish Field.*

The departure of Paine from Guthrie & Wells left a gap which was only filled two years later with the appointment of **Charles Lamb Davidson** as a regular freelance designer. Davidson hailed from Brechin in Angus where his father was a master stonemason. A recruit in the Great War, he had been gassed and invalided out. Having recovered, he entered Glasgow School of Art, where he studied painting and design under **Maurice Greiffenhagen**, Anning Bell and Alexander Walker. By 1925 he was designing for Guthrie & Wells on a regular basis, working mainly from home. Perhaps his earliest designs for the firm are his two small, richly coloured memorial windows for Maryhill Crematorium and his (now dispersed) glass for the demolished Maxwell Parish Church in Pollokshields.

Davidson's skills as a designer were also exploited by Guthrie & Wells in a series of decorative painted panels for the **Cadoro Project**, Glasgow, and he also collaborated with the Edinburgh-based designer Isobel Guthrie in the decoration of the Vauxhall Restaurant in Glasgow. Other important commissions included the scheme of decoration for Glasgow's Locarno Ballroom, and in 1938 he was responsible for a large mural in the Hall of Engineering at the Empire Exhibition.

In 1928 Davidson had married **Nina Miller**, a fellow student at the School of Art; although her output was confined largely to watercolours and embroidery the decline of her husband's health during the early 1940s persuaded her to take up stained glass as a means of easing his burden. She quickly became an important addition to the Guthrie & Wells design team. That she was just as talented and individual in her glass as her husband is convincingly demonstrated by the almost complete scheme carried out by her at

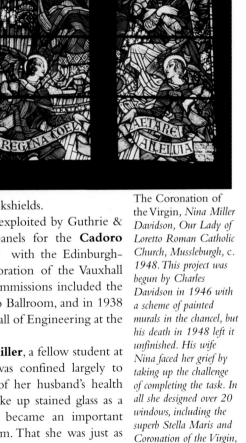

The Coronation of the Virgin, *Nina Miller Davidson, Our Lady of Loretto Roman Catholic Church, Mussleburgh, c. 1948. This project was begun by Charles Davidson in 1946 with a scheme of painted murals in the chancel, but his death in 1948 left it unfinished. His wife Nina faced her grief by taking up the challenge of completing the task. In all she designed over 20 windows, including the superb Stella Maris and Coronation of the Virgin, which form the subjects of the great east window.*

The Lord Forteviot Window *(detail)*, *Charles Baillie, St John's Parish Church, Perth, 1932.*

Our Lady of Loretto Roman Catholic Church in Musselburgh.

Her skill in handling complex and crowded scenes is impressive, and clearly and healthily influenced by Byzantine and Romanesque design. Although her vibrant colours have proven too exuberant for some critics – labels of 'garish and gaudy' have even been applied to them – they are no more so than many contemporary windows by **William Wilson**. It is perhaps their very feminine quality in contrast to the masculinity of her husband's work which has provoked this adverse and insensitive reaction.

Another artist who designed regularly for Guthrie & Wells during the 1920s and 1930s was **Charles Cameron Baillie**. Baillie had trained at Glasgow School of Art under Maurice Greiffenhagen and Anning Bell, both of whom had a powerful influence on his painting style. He had also received practical instruction in stained-glass design by Margaret Chilton and Alexander Strachan. In 1927 he was appointed to succeed Strachan as instructor at Glasgow School of Art when the older man found the pressure of weekly commuting from Edinburgh too much.

Baillie was employed by Guthrie & Wells on a freelance basis from at least 1929. His value to the firm was two-fold. Like Charles Lamb Davidson he was a versatile artist capable of designing both stained glass and murals. He also breathed new life into the almost moribund medium of embossed glass designing in that flowing curvilinear style soon to be christened Art Deco. Baillie moreover had established his own personal contacts with Cunard, P & O and other shipping companies and was securing regular decorative work which could now be carried out under the auspices of the studio.

In domestic work, Baillie tackled everything that came his way, from the peach plate-embossed mirrors in full Art Deco style for the

luxury yacht, the *Queen of Bermuda*, to an entire scheme of decoration and furnishings for Glasgow's Rogano Oyster Bar (1935–6). It was his ability to go on securing regular commissions for ship fitting, even throughout the Depression, which made him such a valued member of the Guthrie & Wells team. In 1935 he installed a scheme of embossed glass in the *Queen Mary* and, like Charles Lamb Davidson, he also executed large-scale murals for the Palace of Industry at the 1938 Exhibition. Although he was still exhibiting from Guthrie & Wells's address in 1958, the latest window thus far identified by him is that depicting St Mungo (1948) formerly in Woodlands Church, Glasgow, and now in the People's Palace collection.

Diana, *Charles Baillie, The Queen of Bermuda yacht, 1933.*

CHAPTER 6

ARTS AND CRAFTS AND THE EAST COAST TRADITION

There is a significant west-coast bias to this study of Scottish glass. This chapter attempts to redress the balance a little by sketching in broad strokes some of the highlights of the lesser known east-coast tradition.

OPPOSITE: *Stair window, William Wilson, Caledonian Insurance Building (now Guardian Financial Services), 13 St Andrews Square, Edinburgh, 1939.*

The concentration on the west-coast stained-glass tradition is understandable since, apart from the work of the Ballantine and Barnett studios, there is little of significance to record on the subject of east-coast design prior to the late 1890s. At that time two commercial studios headed by **W G Boss** and **Nathaniel Bryson** made a brief local flourish. Bryson is known chiefly for his excellent execution of a remarkable Annunciation window in Broughton/St Mary's Church in Edinburgh in 1911. Boss, on the other hand, was evidently a glass stainer of real expertise as can be gauged by the fine window executed by him for the stairs of the Scottish National Portrait Gallery from a design by its architect, **Sir Rowand Anderson**.

The changes in Edinburgh, as in Glasgow, were closely associated with Edinburgh College of Art. In the 1880s and 1890s through the influence and tireless promotion of Patrick Geddes a new grouping of artists emerged with a strongly developed sense of colour in murals, easel painting, sculpture and book illustration. However, only **John Duncan** and Robert Burns out of this important grouping designed for stained glass. Although in both cases their work was of excellent quality it did not significantly impact on the general direction of

The Annunciation, Nathaniel Bryson, Broughton/ St Mary's Church, Edinburgh, 1924.

83

The Children's Window *(detail), John Duncan, Paisley Abbey, 1937.*

Defining the East Coast tradition

When contemporary artists like Douglas Hogg of Edinburgh say they are 'working in the East Coast tradition of Scottish stained glass' they are referring to the work of Douglas Strachan, Herbert Hendrie, Margaret Chilton and William Wilson. Their description does not as a rule include the work of commercial studios like those of Ballantine, Barnett, Nathaniel Bryson and W G Boss. The distinction is not just one of method – arts and crafts versus the division of labour – but also one of style, palette and methodology.

stained-glass design. However, the sympathetic response of both men to the medium was no doubt an important factor in its firm establishment as a subject in Edinburgh College of Art.

Two prolific designers appear briefly in Edinburgh during the 1890s whose main sphere of influence lay in England – **Arthur Louis Duthie** and **William Aikman**. Both contributed designs for stained glass to the Royal Society of Arts in the late 1890s before moving south. Duthie was a skilled church decorator and stained-glass artist who wrote one of the finest textbooks of his generation. Under the title *Decorative Glass Processes* it has been republished in America as a recognised classic. His designs illustrated in the book are very close to the most advanced work of Oscar Paterson and one depicting a Crucifixion is executed entirely in the leadlines with such skill that it would be difficult to find anyone to attempt it today even in copper foil. Aikman enjoyed a very long career as a glass stainer in the Arts and Crafts tradition, and his memorial window to the Scottish missionary, **Mary Slessor**, can be seen in Dundee Museum. However, the work of these artists was of little long-term impact in the capital. It was not until the arrival in town of a young artist from Aberdeen that the domination of the old school began to be seriously challenged. His name was **Douglas Strachan**.

DOUGLAS STRACHAN:
AN ORCHESTRATOR OF COLOUR

Born in Aberdeen in 1875, Douglas Strachan was for a time a student at Gray's School of Art. While still at art school he was accepted as an apprentice lithographer at the *Aberdeen Free Press*. He moved to London and attended the life classes at the Royal Academy. In 1898, after an extensive European tour, he returned to Aberdeen. Initially his reputation was that of a skilled muralist. His earliest glass

(1889) was a window for the lower church in St Nicholas in Aberdeen, where years before, Daniel Cottier's decoration and glass had gone up in flames (see Chapter 2). Strachan was dissatisfied with the result and was only with difficulty persuaded to undertake further commissions. However, within a few years his glass had developed to the point where in technical brilliance it was more than an equal to his earlier achievements in murals.

The early period of his glass can best be seen in the Queen Margaret's College window in the Bute Hall at Glasgow University (1907), where his control of colour, drawing, and technical virtuosity suggest a mind overflowing with good ideas. Strachan's glass began to change in style, colour and materials in the period following the First World War. The impact of that war on him and many other artists was traumatic; gone were the old certainties which had underpinned the craft in the prewar years. Not only had many artists been killed, but many of the dominant ideas which had sustained them had also been weakened. New ideas from France and Italy challenged the Arts and Crafts consensus which had dominated before the war. Movements like **Futurism**, **Cubism**, and **Vorticism** were not only giving rise to new and revolutionary painting styles, but were also challenging the centrality of the human figure in stained glass. Artists like the Dutchman **Johann Thorn Prikker** moved steadily towards abstraction, while in London, **Wyndham Lewis** and the Vorticists, while retaining figures in their compositions, incorporated many of the ideas of the Futurists and Cubists into their own distinctive style.

Strachan was interested in these movements but in terms of his own development they had little impact. Effectively his response to

Perseverance *(detail),*
Douglas Strachan,
Queen Margaret College
window, Bute Hall,
University of Glasgow,
1907.

Douglas Strachan's philosophy

In 1935 the artist was questioned on how he regarded his work in relation to the modernists' form as practised at that moment. Strachan's reply was succinct: 'I don't. And perhaps it would be wisest to continue with 'I wont' and that for two reasons (1) that such an understanding had better be left for others to do: and (2) that I don't know that I could do it if I tried. The fact is that your question shows me, so far as I am aware I have never regarded, compared, or weighed my own works in relation to anything but the image in my head, and the most effective means I could contrive for giving satisfaction to it.'

The Church Triumphant (detail of the great west window), Douglas Strachan, Hyndland Parish Church, Glasgow, 1921.

abstraction was to conceive his windows in terms of areas of pure colour defined and modified by juxtaposition with areas of silvery white. Only once he had achieved this necessary balance would he concentrate on the arrangement and positioning of the subjects. This is a skill in which he was unmatched by any of his generation and displays itself to complete advantage in the many large multi-light and multi-subject compositions which he and Alf Webster alone could orchestrate with such power and conviction. There are so many of these to his credit that it seems almost invidious to single out specific examples, but the east window of Trinity Church, St Andrews (1910), the

Great west window (detail), Douglas Strachan, Hyndland Parish Church, Glasgow, 1921.

five-light window in St Brycedale's Church (now a theatre) in Kirkcaldy (1922–3), the east window in St John's Kirk, Perth (1920), and west window of Hyndland Parish Church (1921) are all splendid examples of this remarkable artist at the height of his powers.

Great east window (detail), Douglas Strachan, Paisley Abbey, 1931.

His most famous work continues to be the scheme for the National War Memorial in Edinburgh Castle, executed in 1925–97 under the supervision of **Sir Robert Lorimer**. All of the glass is rich in symbolic power and anecdotal detail (see Introduction frontispiece). It is the windows in the chancel with their symbolic linking of the soldiers of the Great War with that of Bruce and Bannockburn which reveal Strachan at his most inventive.

EDINBURGH COLLEGE OF ART:
AN UNBROKEN COMMITMENT TO STAINED-GLASS DESIGN

The first impact of the Arts and Crafts ideal of complete control of the process from sketch design to final installation made little impression in Scotland. Christopher Whall's early designs were

St Fillan, *Alexander Strachan, St Fillan's Church, Aberdour, Fife, c. 1930. Alexander Strachan, though less prolific and condemned to live in the shadow of his famous brother, was highly regarded as a brilliant teacher of his medium. His windows, though they are generally small in scale and stylistically very close to his brother's, are nevertheless technically excellent and richly coloured. He is known to have worked regularly as his brother's assistant on large jobs and their work is often confused.*

executed and, no doubt, transmuted by the craftsmen of J & W Guthrie rather than by the hands of the master and his assistants. Slowly, however, as Whall's own glass began to be installed in Scotland at Falkirk (1894) and Douglas Castle Chapel (1896), the reputation of this most influential of artists began to spread. Oscar Paterson was an early member of both the Art Workers' Guild and the Arts and Crafts Society, as was John Guthrie, but the real impact of Whall's influence came in the years immediately preceding and following the Great War.

From 1910 onwards the stained-glass section of the Design Department at Edinburgh College of Art, established by Douglas Strachan, thoroughly entrenched Whall's practices and ideals. Strachan himself was compelled to relinquish his post after a year due to pressure of work with two major schemes of glass for the Free Church College Library, Edinburgh, and the Palace of the Peace at the Hague. However his brother Alexander remained with the School, as instructor, and his students were enabled to participate in the excitement created by these important commissions by occasionally assisting at his brother's studio. This connection with Strachan's studio was a vital one since Edinburgh was conspicuously lacking in the large progressive commercial studios with which Glasgow was so richly endowed.

In 1919 a new Head of Design, **Charles Paine**, was appointed from London. Paine was the ideal recruit; a disciple of Whall and Parsons, he was completely au fait with the best work in the metropolis, particularly Lowndes & Drury. Unfortunately, after only one term he was lured west to Guthrie & Wells and once again the Head of Design was chosen from another discipline. Matters did not improve much until 1923 when two remarkable appointments turned the situation around.

The first was **Gerald Moira** as the new Principal. Since the 1890s Moira had been regarded as one of the foremost muralists in Britain and he had also produced some vigorous designs for stained glass. Shortly after his arrival at the School, he tackled the design deficit created by Paine's abrupt departure by employing the artist and stained-glass designer **Herbert Hendrie**. During his long career at Edinburgh Hendrie combined his teaching role with a large

private practice, which saw him install windows in many parts of Scotland and England. His glass can be seen to advantage at St John's Church, Perth; the Choir of Glasgow Cathedral; St Michael's Church, Linlithgow; and Brechin Cathedral. With his strong personal involvement in stained glass it was natural that Hendrie should seek to enhance the reputation of this section of the School when it was weakened in 1925 by the departure of Alexander Strachan.

For a single term **Mary Wood** attempted to carry on alone but in 1926 she was replaced by Margaret Chilton. Since 1924 Chilton and her former student, Marjorie Kemp, had been running their own joint studio in George Street, Edinburgh, on the strictest Arts and Crafts principles. This did not mean that they were unprepared to execute work to other artists' designs. One of their earliest joint projects was the execution of a window by Robert Burns, the former Head of Painting, for Broughton/St Mary's Church, Edinburgh (1924). As a rule they preferred to work independently, each carrying out their separate windows through all their stages. The arrival of Hendrie and Chilton at the college encouraged many students to regard the medium with new respect. One outstanding young artist, **William Wilson**, who benefited by their encouragement, was to outstrip even Hendrie's burgeoning reputation in Scotland.

Aidan (detail), Mary Wood, St Cuthbert's Parish Church, Edinburgh, 1928. Assistant to Alexander Strachan at Edinburgh College of Art, Mary I Wood was a former student whose drawing, style and palette are significantly looser. She is also known to have collaborated with Douglas Hamilton on several schemes.

WILLIAM WILSON: A MASTER OF COLOUR, DESIGN AND HUMOUR

Born in Edinburgh in 1905, his uncle, Thomas Wilson, had been a designer for Ballantine & Gardener since the 1890s, and was responsible for the remarkable scheme for the Cafe Royal. Under his patronage young William was accepted as an apprentice to **James Ballantine II** in 1920. Like most of Ballantine's apprentices he was encouraged to attend the Art College with a view to improving his drawing skills. During this early period it was printmaking and watercolours which principally engaged his creative energies. For Wilson it was the work of Douglas Strachan which provided the vital spark. In 1928 Strachan began installing his landmark stained-glass scheme in Lorimer's National War Memorial in Edinburgh Castle. Hearing the older – and no doubt jealous – craftsmen in Ballantine's ridiculing Strachan's designs, Wilson went up to see them for himself and was awestruck. Later he recalled that:

Fishermen *(detail of the top stair window)*, William Wilson, *Caledonian Insurance Building, Edinburgh,*

The sheer glassy splendour freed from the sickly yellows and lemonade green [so common in Ballantine's palette] was a revelation. Second only to a first visit to Chartres, it was an experience never to be forgotten.

While he was to remain lavish in his praise of Strachan's glass, singling out the *Te Deum* window in Trinity Church, St Andrews, as being particularly beautiful, Wilson had serious reservations about his later work considering it 'too busy and crowded'. He thought that its 'restlessness in design can sometimes rock the church in which his window becomes too dominating a feature'.

Hendrie's glass by contrast 'while not rising to the imaginative heights of allegory and symbol of Strachan is more successful as stained glass'. Hendrie and Wilson were friends and his close links with Edinburgh Art College, where he had a studio in 1937, would have strengthened that friendship, as well as making the artists very conscious of each other's work. During that year he began a series of 20 panels of stained glass depicting children at play for the Cameron Nursery in Edinburgh's Prestonfield School. In striking contrast to the subject matter of his church glass, Wilson's domestic design, whether for schools, banks or offices, or for personal friends, is always lighthearted, verging on the caricature and never more so than in his delightful windows for the Caledonian Insurance Company in St Andrew's Square, Edinburgh (1939). In them Wilson has left us the finest humorous portrayal of life in and around 'Auld Reekie' (Edinburgh) since John Kay in the 18th century.

The Black Watch War Memorial window, William Wilson, St John's Parish Church, Perth, 1946.

It was in his church work that Wilson's reputation rested and on his remarkable gifts as a colourist, which became more pronounced with the passing of time. His earliest significant work was a single-light window for **Jack Coia's** Roman Catholic Church at the 1938 Empire Exhibition in Glasgow. By the end of the Second World War, Wilson's ecclesiastical style had undergone a dramatic transformation. Some windows for St Andrew's Episcopal Church, Dalkeith, reveal powerfully coloured figure work in an elongated style inspired by Romanesque and Byzantine murals and mosaics.

In 1952 Wilson began his largest and most significant series of windows, for Brechin Cathedral, where virtually every aspect of his changing ideas can be seen. The Queen's Aisle and vestry windows are in his most vigorous and colourful style, with the red-skinned figures which were such a daring innovation in his later work. His great west window of 1958 is by comparison more controlled in its colouring and its drawing, while the clerestory

The Crucifixion, John Macdonald Aitken, Langstane Kirk, Aberdeen, c. 1941.

windows, which are his own personal gift, are in a looser free style much closer to his domestic work.

In 1960 as a result of diabetes he tragically lost his sight. He continued the studio for as long as possible with **John Blyth** as his chief draughtsman. When in 1971 he gave up and moved to Bury in Lancashire his departure was deeply felt, yet such is the fickle nature of fame that on his death in March 1972 the *Glasgow Herald* devoted two column inches to his obituary, and Life and Work made no comment on his passing. John Blyth established his own studio at Balbirnie, in Fife, where he continued to work well into the late 1980s.

Much research still remains to be done into the designs of Walter Pritchard and Sax Shaw, whose work as tutors in glass, mosaics and tapestry contributed so much to sustain Edinburgh's leading role.

Two other artists whose main contribution lay in other areas have nevertheless made significant contributions to stained-glass design. The first of these was **John M Aitken** of Aberdeen, a pupil of Gerald Moira at the Royal College in London. He had a long and distinguished career as a painter and was for a time (1911–1914) Principal of Gray's School of Art, Aberdeen. In 1941 at the age of 61 he began a remarkable scheme of stained glass for the Langstane Kirk, in Union Street, Aberdeen. Aitken's powerful draughtsmanship and colour control in this scheme would be remarkable in a young

man; as a late flowering it is truly exceptional. The range and number of his other works in stained glass is currently unknown but a forthcoming publication on these windows will help to stimulate further research.

The great west window (detail), Ralph Cowan, Broom Parish Church, Newton Mearns, 1958.

Ralph Cowan from Glasgow has also had a long and distinguished career as an architect and a painter, as well as serving as Head of Architecture at Edinburgh College of Art (1948–53 and 1956–78). As early as the 1930s he was experimenting in both stained and embossed glass, but it his windows, particularly two exuberant and daringly modern designs for Broom Parish Church, Newton Mearns (1958), which provide in stained glass a perfect complement to the contemporary symbolism and colour schemes of his late colleague **Sir Robin Philipson**. Like Philipson, Cowan is first and foremost a colourist and his exuberant depiction of rich arabesques of daringly formalised plants, flowers, birds and fish have the same uninhibited bravura that one finds in the very best work of J D Fergusson. Any future history of Scottish art which fails to include his glass would be sadly flawed.

CHAPTER 7

'THE TERRIBLE CRYSTAL'

ADVENTURES IN *DALLES DE VERRE*

After the death of Alf Webster the initiative in glass staining passed from Glasgow to the east coast and Douglas Strachan. In spite of the many fine artists who worked in the west coast during the intervening years, it was not until the early 1960s that Edinburgh's supremacy was to be challenged and challenged significantly, in a male-dominated craft, by a woman, Sadie McLellan.

Although Glasgow seemed to be resting on its laurels, it should not be assumed that Guthrie & Wells were alone in sustaining its reputation during the 1930s and 1940s. In spite of the collapse of William Meikle and Oscar Paterson, other firms, like J P McPhie, the **City Glass Company** and the St Enoch's Glass Company, continued to provide good-quality stained glass. Andrew Rigby Gray moved to McPhie and continued to design for them on a regular basis. Marcus McLundie's City Glass Company also developed a high reputation for embossed glass and *vitriolite* work for cafés, restaurants and domestic bathrooms.

THE LEGACY OF ALF WEBSTER

The chief competition came from Alf Webster's widow, M C M Webster who continued to operate her dead husband's firm under its original title of the Stephen Adam Studio. In 1929 it finally passed under the direct management of Alf's son **Gordon MacWhirter Webster** who had been an infant at the time of his father's death. Mrs Webster had managed to keep the studio solvent by placing the practical management of the glass shop in the hands of the firm's former apprentice and assistant **Douglas Hamilton**.

OPPOSITE: Christian struggling with Apollyon, *Sadie McLellan, The Robin Chapel, Thistle Foundation, Craigmillar, Edinburgh, 1952. One of eight windows by McLellan which tell the tale of Christian from the Pilgrim's Progress. They present an extraordinary gallery of bold and exciting images from the almost barbarous sensuality of Vanity Fair to this elemental struggle between Christian and Satan, presented as a green-bodied, purple-winged Behemoth licked by flames.*

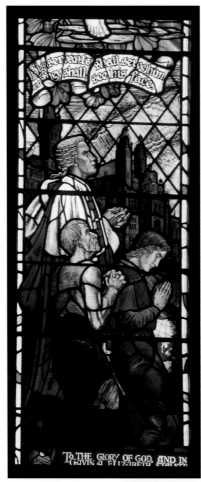

His Servants Shall
Serve Him, *Douglas
Hamilton, Hyndland
Parish Church, Glasgow,*
c. *1930.*

Christ in Majesty,
*Gordon Webster, St
Mary's Parish Church,
Peel Street, Glasgow,
c. 1968 (now in People's
Palace collection).*

Hamilton in turn drew upon the design assistance of freelance artists like Alexander Walker, David Gauld and possibly Ancell Stronach. It is clear that Hamilton was Alf Webster's close assistant and was able to complete several of his commissions which were outstanding at the time of his death. His own designs are often inspired by Alf Webster's compositional ideas, most notably the large three-light window in Hyndland Parish Church, Glasgow, where the architecture of Glasgow Art Gallery and Glasgow University provides a background for a window celebrating 'Service'.

Gordon McWhirter Webster was trained by Hamilton, but like him he was for a number of years strongly influenced by his late father's work. His fine early window (1931) in the Parish Church at Helensburgh might very well be mistaken for that of his father's. However by the mid-1930s he had discovered his own voice and some of his work of this period is very fine indeed, particularly the windows in St Columba's Parish Church in Largs. Favoured by the Church of Scotland, his output was prolific. One of his best works, a great rose window depicting *Christ in Majesty* from St Mary's Church Partick, is now in the People's Palace collection, and was a focal point in the Interdenominational Church at the Glasgow Garden Festival, 1988.

Another designer who somewhat reluctantly began designing for glass in Glasgow but moved to Edinburgh in 1940 was **R Douglas McLundie**.

Born in 1908, he attended the Slade School of Art in London from 1926 to 1929. He returned to Glasgow, where he entered the family business, the City Glass Company, founded by his grandfather. There in the stained-glass shop of that commercial studio he was taught glass painting by the **George Neil**, a veteran of the craft who had worked successively for Stephen Adam, Oscar Paterson, and Guthrie & Wells, and was regarded as the finest glass painter in the city. In 1940 McLundie and his family moved to Edinburgh, where he took over the management of the Edinburgh branch of the firm operating under the title 'The Abbey Studio' in the Grassmarket. In 1964 McLundie closed the studio and retired to the Isle of Seil but died shortly afterwards.

SADIE McLELLAN:
A PASSIONATE QUEST FOR PERFECTION

One challenging artist who emerged in the 1930s, Sadie F McLellan, has produced an exceptional body of work. A perfectionist by temperament, working always in solitary conditions, her output has been significantly smaller than her contemporaries such as Wilson and Webster, yet it contains some of the most powerful and imaginative glass in 20th-century Scotland.

Noah, *R Douglas McLundie, Abbey Studio, Edinburgh, for Alloway Parish Church, c. 1950.*

Born in Glasgow in 1912, her father, an idealistic socialist, recognised and encouraged her talent and that of her brother Robert, who became a distinguished playwright and author. Her teacher at Bearsden Academy, the artist William Armour, persuaded her to enter Glasgow School of Art. In 1931 in her third year she first entered the stained-glass studio of Charles Baillie and was deeply impressed by the possibilities and challenge of the medium. Her own draughtsmanship and sense of colour were already well developed, and her post-diploma panel, depicting Mary Queen of Scots, though

The Humiliation and Death of Christ, *Sadie McLellan, Church of the Sacred Heart, Cumbernauld, 1964–5. Amid the carefully contrived mystical gloom of the deep blue walls, these searingly rendered and powerfully symbolic images have a hypnotic intensity which must have astonished the original congregation, and their power to move the beholder remains undiminished. Like the pulsating graph on a life support machine, the glass records in vertical bands of blood red, white, ochre and blue the torment, passion, and death of Christ.*

clearly influenced by Baillie, shows a remarkable assurance and an absolute mastery of the medium. Awarded the John Keppie travelling scholarship, she spent a year at the Danish Royal Academy of Art at **Copenhagen**, where she produced several designs for windows, including a three-light memorial for a crematorium. She also executed her first full commission, four domestic panels illustrating the zodiac for a house in Fredensborg.

When her cartoons were returned to the School for exhibition they created a sensation, and, in spite of the publicity blitz on the forthcoming coronation, were published with a glowing review in the Glasgow *Evening News*. McLellan's first palpable success came in 1938 when she contributed a mural, an engraved glass panel and a stained-glass window to the Women's Pavilion at the Empire Exhibition.

In 1940 she met and married **Walter Pritchard**, the stained-glass artist and muralist who was tutor in the Design Department at Edinburgh College of Art, while she herself joined the design staff of Glasgow School of Art from 1940 to 1945.

Stylistically McLellan's glass falls into two distinct periods. The first begins with two large transept windows for Balshagray Parish Church, Glasgow (1948), where her bold and distinctive figure work has already moved dramatically away from the almost Pre-Raphaelite detail of her diploma panel. Three years later the two choir windows in Glasgow Cathedral, particularly the richly coloured north window, proclaim in unmistakable fashion the arrival of a major new talent. Her competition design for the great west window was rejected. However, Glasgow's loss was Edinburgh's gain; through the patronage of Lord Maufe, McLellan was given the commission to design a complete scheme of glass for the newly built Robin Chapel of the Thistle Foundation at Craigmillar, Edinburgh (1951–4).

Christopher Whall when listening to descriptions of the latest works of his students was wont to query impatiently 'Yes! Yes! but do the colours sing?' In this Robin Chapel scheme McLellan's glass sings with all the emotional intensity of an aria by Maria Callas or a spiritual by Mahalia Jackson (Chapter frontispiece). Other works like the superb *Te Deum* in Belmont Parish Church, Glasgow, sustained the momentum. In 1958 McLellan while on holiday made an exciting trip from the south of France to see the revolutionary new glass completed in 1952 at **Audincourt** by **Fernand Léger**. The impact of these major windows in a new medium *(dalles de verre)* was overwhelming. Writing in 1997 McLellan states unequivocally that the Léger windows at Audincourt are 'the finest modern windows in the world'. With the single-minded assurance that permeates that opinion, McLellan returned to Scotland determined to spread the revolution. A period of intense experimentation followed resulting in the creation of six exceptional panels. Only two now remain in Scotland – a moving and exquisitely coloured Pietà, now in the collection of the National Museums of Scotland, and a rich sensuously Picasso-esque essay entitled *The Lover* in a private collection in Glasgow.

In 1960 she carried out her first public commission for dalles de verre at Alloa Parish Church with the installation of a three-light window. The first large-scale window in this medium to be tackled by McLellan came in 1962 when she undertook to design and install glazing for the north transept of the medieval Benedictine Priory of **Pluscarden**, near Elgin, in Moray. The chief feature of this great window of three tall lancets was a very large rose, for which McLellan designed an extraordinary panel depicting the following scene from the Book of Revelations:

> and there appeared a great wonder in Heaven, a woman clothed
> with the sun, and the moon under her feet, and upon her had a crown
> of twelve stars . . . And there appeared another wonder in heaven;
> behold a great red dragon . . . and his tail drew the third part of the
> stars of heaven, and it cast them to the earth.

The panel itself was enormous and when it was exhibited in Edinburgh in sections it caused enormous excitement. The design was one of great power and originality and took the better part of two years to complete, the concrete support being deliberately

Dalles de Verre

Unlike traditional stained glass, the glass used in dalles de verre is made in moulds producing slabs of one inch or more in thickness. These slabs are cut or chipped into manageable pieces using a special tungsten hammer and anvil. The pieces are then bedded in cement or an alternative resin and allowed to set. When reinforced with metal rods, entire walls of glass (as at Audincourt) can be formed, producing in the 20th century an equivalent to the kind of liberation felt in the 13th century with the invention of the flying buttress.

Casting dice for His garments, *Sadie McLellan, Church of The Sacred Heart, Cumbernauld, 1964–5.*

modelled externally to compensate for the lack of medieval tracery. However, to test this new medium to its full potential a new building was required. The opportunity came in 1964 when McLellan collaborated with the veteran architect Jack Coia, and his two associates **Isi Metzstein** and **Andy MacMillan**, in the building of the Church of the Sacred Heart at Cumbernauld. One of a series of post-modern churches built by Coia and his associates in the 1960s, it was rectangular in shape and, unlike the others, severely plain externally. This gave McLellan the unusual opportunity of making her dalles de verre the chief decorative feature of both the exterior and interior of the church.

Other notable schemes in both dalles de verre, at Orchardhill Parish Church, Glasgow, and in stained glass, at Cardonald Parish Church, Glasgow, and at Hurlford Parish Church (1969) and

The Crucifixion, *Sadie McLellan, Cardonald Parish Church, Glasgow, c.1961.*

Netherlee (1969), provide convincing evidence of McLellan's pre-eminence in her chosen medium.

Such is the timidity of our architectural profession that what should have been a glorious new beginning for architectural stained glass remains a solitary but inspiring challenge to future generations. While the indefatigable McLellan continued to experiment with free-standing glass sculpture (Cherry Bank Garden, Perth, 1979), no new opportunities in dalles de verre were forthcoming. In 1989 she completed her final work in Scotland, an exuberant interpretation of Teilhard de Chardin's *Hymn to the Universe* in the Martyrs' Church, St Andrews, and quietly retired to live with her architect daughter in Canada. **Hugh MacDiarmid's** poem *The Terrible Crystal* was dedicated McLellan in admiration of her indomitable personality and remarkable achievements.

THE PRECARIOUS PRESENT

With the death of Gordon Webster and the retirement of Sadie McLellan in 1991 an uncertain era in Scottish stained glass began. Unlike the situation in the 1890s, the 1990s and the next century do not seem to offer new promise for those artists attempting to earn a precarious living in stained glass.

Some threads of the great traditions outlined in previous chapters still survive. Some veterans like **Crear McCartney** enjoy a fair amount of patronage. McCartney was a pupil of Walter Pritchard at Glasgow School of Art in the 1950s and as his early single-light window in St Peter's Roman Catholic Church in Partick clearly demonstrates he was for a time heavily influenced by his old master. However by the early 1960s he had evolved his own distinctive style in which boldly coloured plant and floral motifs predominate. A particularly fine example of his work in this vein, consisting of elaborate medieval style foliage patterns of superbly painted passion flowers, can be seen in the Church of Scotland, Auchtermuchty. More recently McCartney has carried out several major windows for important historic churches such as **St Michael's**, Linlithgow, and **Holy Rude**, Stirling.

At Edinburgh Art College, **Douglas Hogg** was one of **Roland Sax Shaw's** most gifted pupils of the 1960s. Since the late 1970s, he has maintained the high

OPPOSITE: The Unification window, *John Clark, Oakshaw/Trinity Parish Church, Paisley, 1996. John Clark stands out as a new superstar of Scottish stained glass. His style and use of colour have been dramatically affected by his international perspective and the early naturalism of his shoal of fish for the windows of the Café Gandolfi, and his parakeet and cockatoos for Princes Square have now given way to the bold symbolism and colour of his Glasgow Synagogue scheme, and his adventurous new designs for the Scottish Piping College, and Strathclyde University's Barony Church building (both in Glasgow) in which monochromatic colour schemes of blue or red allied to complex symbology predominate.*

The Phoenix *(detail), Roland Sax Shaw, Hyndland Parish Church, 1969.*

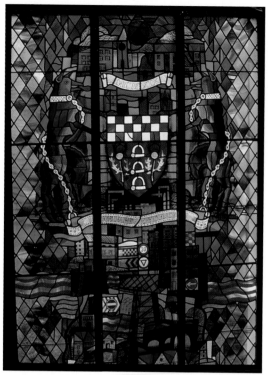

Scottish Police Federation window, Alfredo Avella, Woodside Terrace, Glasgow, 1977.

The Dove, John Clark, 1982 (Glasgow Museums: Art Gallery & Museum, Kelvingrove).

standards and enthusiasm for stained glass so long associated with that institution. He has always been a supreme colourist, working in what he would call the 'Scottish east coast tradition'. But Hogg has always been his own man and his bold semi-abstract symbolism allied to a great virtuosity of technique has deservedly placed him among the most outstanding of our contemporary designers. His earliest commissioned designs for stained glass were featured on STV's *Encore for the Arts* programme in 1981, in a rare, almost exceptional in-depth interview with a living artist in this publicity-starved medium. Since 1972, when his first windows were installed at **Thornton Parish Church** in Fife, Hogg, while inspiring a host of students, has produced a commendable body of work.

By contrast, Glasgow School of Art has continued to produce outstanding practitioners in stained glass almost in spite of itself. Since the untimely death of **Alfredo Avella** in 1981 stained glass has been firmly marginalised and is now reduced to the level of a part-time hobby course outwith the main curriculum. Avella's death occurred ironically on the eve of the 1981 exhibition, 'Glasgow Stained Glass', at the People's Palace, which for the first time chronicled Glasgow's unique role as a centre of stained-glass design and production.

Avella himself was primarily a muralist and had only a handful of windows to his credit, yet his enthusiasm was enough to launch the careers of **John Clark**, whose spectacularly successful

104

development has mirrored those of his near contemporaries **Adrian Wiszniewski**, **Steven Campbell**, **Ken Currie** and **Peter Howson** in painting. Others of Avella's students, **Shona McInnes**, **Susan Laidler** and **Eidlith Keith**, are all still practising their art. Yet only Clark has been able to establish an international reputation for his work and recently has had to move to Germany to secure the kind of architectural and critical support habitually lavished on the successful painter. Most of our best young artists, such as **Susan Bradbury** and **Paul Lucky**, **Ericka Shovelin**, **Emma Butler-Cole Aitken**, **Emma Shipton**, **Britta Sugden**, **Laura Bentley** and **Christian Shaw**, must continue to support themselves by conservation work, the occasional memorial window and that most ephemeral of outlets for stained glass, shop fitting. Sadly neither John Clark nor any of the other artists cited in this chapter have ever featured in the many published works on contemporary Scottish art.

The Forrest, Susan Laidler, St John's Church Centre, Bath Street, Glasgow, 1986.

The Robert Burns Memorial, Susan Bradbury, Alloway Parish Church, Ayrshire, 1996.

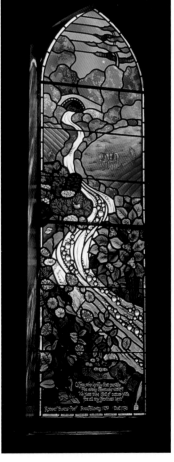

None of the new Glasgow painters of the 1980s tried their hand at stained glass, and given the lack of incentive, it is unlikely that any will do so in the future. It is however not only the schools but the architectural profession which must shake off the loss of resolve occasioned by the collapse of confidence in post-modern architecture. The supporting arts of sculpture, murals, stained glass and mosaic are as vital to any worthwhile architecture of the future as they have been in the past. We neglect any or all of them at our cost. In order to have new glass we must have new buildings, where the glass is an essential part of the architectural whole, not a last minute add on. One important new building to contain a specially commissioned window is the new **Museum of Scotland**, Edinburgh, where a window by Crear McCartney, gifted by the Society of Antiquaries of

LEFT: The Factor's transportation list, *Yvonne Smith and Joe Boyle, The Lismore Bar, Partick, Glasgow, 1997. A fine modern panel but the restraints of working in a historicist style are apparent when compared with their contemporary screen for Page and Park's Italian Centre, Glasgow, which displays in design and technique a freshness and originality which Oscar Paterson would have admired.*

RIGHT: *Into the next millennium – design for a stained-glass window for the new Museum of Scotland, Crear McCartney, 1997. This window, a gift from the Society of Antiquaries of Scotland, was commissioned to commemorate the historic and continuing links between the Society and the National Museums. McCartney has encompassed in colour, texture and detail the rich range of material held by the museum from the earliest prehistoric pottery and metalwork to Roman inscriptions, a Christian crozier and the Society's Charter and arms.*

Scotland, will display the finest of Scotland's stained-glass tradition in a modern setting. This should not be an isolated example: without the committed support of the architectural profession stained glass is an art with nowhere to go.

The late Hugh MacDiarmid was often heard exasperatedly proclaiming that in matters cultural the chief vice of the Scots was low aim. It is to be hoped that the impetus provided by a Scottish Parliament will result in greater opportunities for innovation both in architecture and stained glass which can and should avoid that vice. If this book can induce in architects, artists, patrons and the general public a new awareness of the past achievements and future potential of this most colourful of architectural arts, it will have succeeded.

GLOSSARY

Antique glass: a 19th-century term for hand-made, blown glass, made in imitation of the medieval with characteristic irregular texture

Arts and Crafts movement: in relation to glass, this refers to the complete abandonment of division of labour so that each window is designed, constructed and installed by the same artist

Art Nouveau: originating with Samuel Bing's 'Galleries de l'Art Nouveau' in Paris, the term became a generic one for the new movement in decorative art in France, based in particular on stylised plant motifs, and its Scottish counterpart, the Glasgow Style

Calm: grooved, H-sectioned strap of lead used to hold and join individual pieces of glass

Cartoon: full-sized paper design for window or panel

Crown glass: glass spun into a large disc before being removed from the glass-blower's rod or pontil, leaving the characteristic pontil mark

Dalles de verre: pieces of slab glass, usually about one inch thick, often chipped or faceted on the surface which are set into concrete or epoxy resin

Embossed glass: commonly used term for sand-blasted or etched glass where the areas removed by abrasion produce a raised effect, similar to that achieved on leather by the pressure of a dye

Ferramenta: wrought-iron framework used to support the complex panels forming a large medieval window

Flashed glass: two-layered glass, usually white with a thin layer of a darker colour, often ruby red, blue or green, above it

Foil: small arc opening in Gothic tracery with the number of foils indicated by a prefix: e.g. quatrefoil - four arcs

Grisaille: panels of predominantly silvery white glass, painted with delicate geometric or floral designs, with much cross-hatching and few or no coloured highlights

Grozing: trimming technique whereby complex glass shapes can be obtained with the use of a grozing iron, a hooked tool that leaves a characteristic nibbled edge

Lancet: tall thin pointed window

Leading up: process of soldering together the lead calms and individual pieces of glass of a window, after completion of painting and staining

Leadlines: dominant lines of the design produced by the shapes of the lead calmes containing individual glass pieces

Light: opening between the mullions of a window with the number of lights indicated by a prefix: single-, two-, three-light, etc.; windows can range from a tiny single-light one-panel window, to a 10- or 12-light window with 48 separate panels and additional tracery

Medallion windows: windows (e.g. at Chartres, St Chapelle and Canterbury) composed of variously shaped small panels often arranged in a narrative sequence

Muff, or cylinder, glass: glass produced by cutting off the end of an elongated balloon of glass which is then split along its length to form a flattened sheet

Opalescent glass: glass developed in the late 19th century by John La Farge and later popularised by Tiffany in which streaks of colour, when fused, give a milky iridescent appearance

Pot metal: antique glass coloured throughout with one colour

Quarry glass: square or diamond-shaped pane of white or green glass used to provide conveniently assembled backdrops to the main subject of a window; often decorated with birds, insects and flowers

Saddle bars: flat or round bars of iron used to support the window, normally positioned across the joint between two of the panels forming a window

Slab glass: thick flat glass of a single colour

Stippling: method of painting in many tiny dots which creates the effect of minute points of light over designated portions of the glass

Ties: lengths of copper wire attached at strategic points to the top and bottom edges of a stained glass panel at its junction another panel, twisted around the saddle bar to anchor the window securely in place

INDEX OF ARTISTS

INDEX OF STAINED-GLASS LOCATIONS

FURTHER READING

A number of books give general introductions to stained glass:
Brown, Sarah, *Stained Glass: An Illustrated History* (London, 1994); Harrison, Martin, *Victorian Stained Glass* (London, 1980); Reyntiens, Patrick, *The Beauty of Stained Glass* (London, 1990); Sturm, James L, *Stained Glass from Mediæval Times to the Present: Treasures to be seen in New York* (New York, 1982); Biographies of individuals and groups are numerous although there are still few on purely Scottish artists: Bilcliffe, Roger, *Charles Rennie Mackintosh: Furniture and Interiors* (London, 1979) and *The Glasgow Boys* (John Murray; 1985). Burkhauser, Jude, *The Glasgow Girls: Women in Art and Design* (Edinburgh, 1990); Cormack, Peter, *Women Stained-glass Artists of the Arts and Crafts Movement* (London, 1985), also *Henry Holiday* (London, 1989), *Christopher Whall* (London, 1979) and *Karl Parsons* (London, 1987); Moon, Karen, *George Walton* (London, 1993). A further three titles which have contributed greatly to this book: Pearson, Fiona, *William Wilson* (Edinburgh 1994); Rawson, George, *Fra Newbery* (Glasgow 1996) and Buchanan, William, 'The Terrible Crystal: The Work of Sadie McLellan' (*Scottish Art Review* 1973).
Finally, the writings of the early practitioners give further insights:
Adam, Stephen, *Truth in Decorative Art* (Glasgow, 1896); Ballantine, James, *A Treatise on Painted Glass* (Edinburgh, 1845); Whall, Christopher, *Stained Glass Work* (London, 1905).

SELECTIVE LIST OF SITES TO VISIT

Throughout the book locations of individual windows and panels (indexed on pp. 109–111) have been given as a guide of where to see Scottish stained glass. The publication *Churches to Visit in Scotland* (Scotland's Churches Scheme, 1997) will give further information. Just as Scottish stained glass has enriched public buildings and churches all over the world, so Scotland has in its turn benefited from the talents of non-Scots designers in stained glass; in this section we list a some outstanding examples of these which are well worth visiting.

Leifur Breidfjord of Iceland
The Robert Burns Memorial,
   St Giles' Kirk, Edinburgh

Harry Clarke
Notre Dame Convent, Bearsden,
   Glasgow

Louis Davis
Dunblane Cathedral, Stirlingshire
All Saints, St Andrews, Fife
St John's Church, Perth

Henry Holiday
Dunfermline Abbey, Fife
The Bute Hall, Glasgow University
Brechin Cathedral, Angus
St Leonard's Church, St Andrews, Fife

C E Kempe
Govan Old Parish Church, Glasgow
Paisley Abbey, Renfrewshire
St Giles' Kirk, Edinburgh

Gabriel Loire of Chartres
Church of the Holy Name, Oakley, Fife

William Morris / Sir Edward Burne-Jones
Kirkcaldy Old Parish Church
The Bute Hall, Glasgow University

King's College Chapel, Aberdeen
The Old West Kirk, Greenock
St Giles' Kirk, Edinburgh
Bothwell Parish Church
The People's Palace Museum, Glasgow
The Museum of Religion, Glasgow

Keith New
Glasgow University Chapel

Karl Parsons
Paisley Abbey, Renfrewshire
All Saints Episcopal, St Andrews, Fife
St Giles' Kirk, Edinburgh
Old St Paul's Episcopal, Edinburgh

Pat Pollen of Tur na Gloine, Dublin
Rosslyn Chapel, Lothian

Louis Comfort Tiffany
Tiffany's Cafe (Carnegie Hall),
   Dunfermline, Fife
St Cuthbert's Parish Church, Edinburgh
Fyvie Parish Church, Aberdeenshire

Christopher W Whall
The Clark Memorial Church, Largs
Falkirk Parish Church, Stirlingshire
The People's Palace Museum, Glasgow

Printed in Scotland for The Stationery Office Limited
J26827, C30, 11/97, CCN 056901.